CONTENTS

Ships in Focus Publications
Correspondence and editorial:
Roy Fenton
18 Durrington Avenue
London SW20 8NT
020 8879 3527
rfenton@rfenton.demon.co.uk
Orders and photographic:
John & Marion Clarkson
18 Franklands, Longton
Preston PR4 5PD
01772 612855
sales@shipsinfocus.co.uk
© 2001 Individual contributors,
John Clarkson and Roy Fenton.

Printed by Amadeus Press
Ltd., Cleckheaton, Yorkshire.
Designed by Hugh Smallwood,
John Clarkson and Roy Fenton.
SHIPS IN FOCUS RECORD
ISBN 1 901703 14 2

SHIPS IN FOCUS

Following our foray into the wo
bankruptcy) in our last issue, *Reco*
room and returns to more familiar
those who admire British cargo ships, especially the classics of
post-war years. However, there is one difference: a 16-page
colour section. As explained in the last issue, a historical journal
such as this need not be held back by an adherence to black and
white photography, but several articles we wanted to feature (on
flags and funnels, for instance) simply cried out for colour. We
are also aware that history ended very recently, and the wealth of
colour transparencies taken since the 1960s means it has been
possible to illustrate the article on *Wellington Star* entirely in
colour, doing full justice to the attractive and well-kept ships of
Blue Star. In addition, we cannot ignore trends in publishing,
with even the 'Economist' adopting colour! We will continue the
experiment of a colour section in *Record* 18.

The offices of Ships in Focus have been much occupied
lately with an extended publication programme, and one result is
our first history of a shipbuilder, 'Philip and Son Ltd.,
Shipbuilders and Engineers' by Derek Blackhurst. Amongst
almost 1,500 completions, Philips produced an enormous variety
of craft. Derek has completed the histories of all the substantial
craft built at Dartmouth, and we believe this is one of the first
yard lists to give such detail. As always, *Record* subscribers have
a special offer on the book: see opposite.

In case there is any misunderstanding regarding the
subscription rates we published in *Record* 16, we should point out
that short-term, three-issue subscriptions are still available at
existing and advantageous rates. However, even more substantial
savings are available to those taking out six- or nine-issue
subscriptions, as detailed below.

John Clarkson   Roy Fenton
July 2001

SUBSCRIPTION RATES FOR RECORD

Subscribers make a saving on postage, and receive each *Record* just as
soon as it is published. They are also eligible for concessions on
newly-published *Ships in Focus* titles. Readers can start their
subscription with *any* issue, and are welcome to backdate it to receive
previous issues.

	3 issues	6 issues	9 issues
UK	£23	£44	£63
Europe (airmail)	£25	£47	£68
Rest of world (surface mail)	£25	£47	£68
Rest of world (airmail)	£30	£56	£81

Wellington Star (see page 34 onwards). *[Fotoflite incorporating Skyfotos]*

Fleet in Focus

THE FURNESS GOALPOSTERS
David Burrell

The years during and after the First World War saw Furness, Withy and Co. Ltd. change character. Apart from investment in Houlders, prewar they had been owners of cargo and tramp tonnage, along with shipyards, coal, iron and steel. The purchase of the Johnston, Prince and Rio Cape Lines, plus Bermuda, turned the company into major liner operators. The existing shipyards were sold in 1917 and 1918 and a new yard built at Haverton Hill-on-Tees. The major change was the 1919 management buyout which left Haverton Hill, the coal, iron and steel interests with the Furness family and the shipping assets with a company led by Frederick Lewis, who later became Lord Essendon.

The fleet suffered badly in the war, and the 88 ships sunk needed replacement. Prior to the buyout, Lord Furness placed many orders with yards at high wartime prices. Renegotiation of these was imperative, and failure could bankrupt the company. Typical were no fewer than 44 orders at Haverton Hill, which were reduced by Lewis to 26, of which 24 were actually delivered.

Building at the Tees yard was a class of six 450-foot shelter deckers. Delivered from May 1922 to December 1923, they loaded over 11,000 tons and featured distinctive goalpost masts. 4,600 SHP geared turbines drove single screws, giving 14 knots. Like many cargo liners they berthed 12 passengers.

First delivered was *Feliciana*. Her renaming as *London Mariner* is a reminder of the variety of nomenclatures used by the company. In the Victorian era the suffix *-City* was widely used. In the 1890s came the suffix *-iana*, often attached to names of countries and places. Briefly post-1918 the prefix *London* was used and applied to five of this class.

Originally, Manchester Liners were to take three of the class, but high prices meant they took only one, destined to be the only member of the class to remain with her original owners throughout her life.

Ownership of the five London boats rested with various Group companies. Furness, Withy itself had *Feliciana*, *London Importer* and *London Commerce*. In 1923 *Feliciana* passed to Gulf Line Ltd. as *London Mariner*, only to return to Furness, Withy in 1929. Neptune Steam Navigation Co. Ltd. had *London Merchant* and Norfolk and North American Steam Ship Co. Ltd. the *London Shipper*. As their *London* names suggest, the ships ran from the Thames to the east and west coasts of the USA.

The decade following the war was a bad one for shipping, and the Wall Street Crash of 1929 heralded even worse. The USA withdrew foreign loans, and imports dried up. The world followed the USA into the Great Depression. The consequence for the London boats was dire. With their inflated building costs, fuel-hungry turbines (to provide the speed thought necessary on this prestigious and competitive route), and fierce and subsidised competition for cargoes, they were simply too large and too expensive. When withdrawn from the North Atlantic in 1929, three were renamed for charter to Prince Line, but without change of registered owners. As even this employment opportunity dried up all five were laid up in the Blackwater, off Tollesbury. *Lloyd's Shipping Index* for December 1932 recorded their arrivals, *London Merchant* on 12th April 1930 followed by *Imperial Prince* (10th September 1930), *British Prince* (12th December 1930), *Royal Prince* (15th May 1931) and *London Importer* (22nd June 1931).

Last in, first out, *London Importer* was sold to the Admiralty on 24th March 1933 for £46,000 to become the Fleet Supply Ship *Reliant*. In 1935 the four remaining were sold for even less: knocked down for £123,000 for the lot to Thos. & Jas. Harrison, who spent the 1930s on the lookout for bargains.

Opposite: the infamous *Politician* in the Mersey.
Below: *Feliciana*, first of the series
(see next page).

Four of the group were lost during the war, the return of peace finding only *Collegian* ex-*London Commerce* and *Reliant* ex-*London Importer* afloat. The former went to the breakers in 1948, but after sale to Pakistan the *Reliant* lasted until 1963. Hardly beauties, their goalpost masts, large superstructure and big upright funnel nevertheless gave them an impressive appearance, which seems to have particularly suited the colour scheme of Harrisons.

LONDON MARINER (upper), **IMPERIAL PRINCE** (lower) and **CRAFTSMAN** (opposite top)
Furness Shipbuilding Co. Ltd., Haverton Hill-on-Tees; 1922, 7,896gt, 472 feet
Two single-reduction geared turbines by John Brown and Co. Ltd., Clydebank.
The first of these turbine steamers was delivered in May as *Feliciana* (see previous page), reflecting a naming scheme used by Furness since the mid-1890s. But even this name was an afterthought, as there is evidence that she was launched, on 21st June 1921, with the Johnston Warren name *Rowanmore*. *Feliciana*, as she became before completion, was renamed *London Merchant* on transfer to Furness' Gulf Line in December 1922. Despite some good

passages - these turbine driven ships could exceed their nominal 14 knots when pushed - competition on the London to east coast USA route ultimately proved too much, and in late 1929 *London Mariner* was transferred to Prince Line, becoming *Imperial Prince*. But this was only a stopgap and, in the face of a deepening trade depression, she was laid up in the River Blackwater, arriving on 10th September 1930.

After almost five years' idleness, four of the group were bought by T. and J. Harrison Ltd. of Liverpool, a company which was cannily taking advantage of the recession by buying up some excellent tonnage at bargain prices. They acquired the four Furness goalposters for about a

quarter of what they had cost to build.

The one-time *London Mariner* became *Craftsman*. Along with two of her sisters, she was not to survive the Second World War, and was sunk by the German auxiliary cruiser KMS *Kormoran* on 9th April 1941. *Craftsman* was on a voyage from Rosyth to Table Bay with a cargo which included a net defence system for Cape Town harbour. She came up to the raider about 800 miles west of Dakar, and was heavily shelled, causing the loss of six men, the remainder being taken prisoner whilst demolition charges were set, although it still required a torpedo to finish her off. *[Upper: K.G. Petersen, Eric Johnson collection, courtesy Bill Schell. Middle: R.J. Scott courtesy George Scott]*

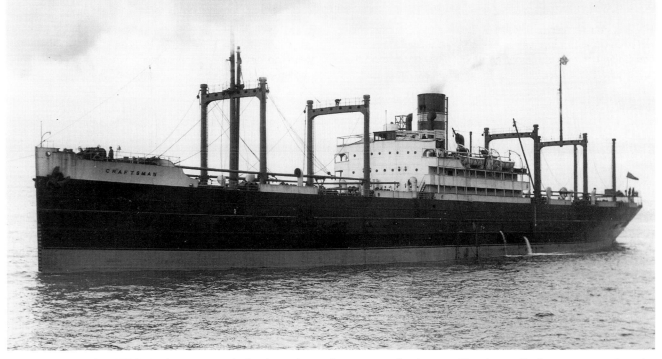

MANCHESTER REGIMENT (below)

Furness Shipbuilding Co. Ltd., Haverton Hill-on-Tees; 1922, 7,930gt 450 feet

Two single-reduction geared turbines by Richardsons, Westgarth and Co. Ltd., Middlesbrough.

Rebuilding their fleet after the First World War, Manchester Liners Ltd. initially agreed to take three of the six goalpost-design turbine steamers. But in view of the price of £458,598, this was reduced to just one.

Not laid up like her sisters in the early 1930s, *Manchester Regiment* had nothing if not an eventful career. In December 1929 she answered the distress calls of the *Volumnia* (5,608/1911), sinking in a North Atlantic hurricane. With the help of oil pumped on to the water by the tanker *Saco* (5,106/1919), *Manchester Regiment* launched a boat which made two trips to the *Volumnia* to rescue all 45 members of her crew.

On 23rd October 1937 *Manchester Regiment* rammed the *Clan Mackenzie* (6,554/1917), which was sailing from Liverpool for East London. The Clan Liner was overtaking the Manchester Liner, which was flying the flags 'JI',

indicating that she was adjusting compasses. *Clan Mackenzie* had to be beached and was declared a total loss, being broken up at Troon. In the subsequent court case, the judge ruled that fault lay 80% with *Manchester Regiment*.

Her second collision was to have much direr consequences. South west of Cape Race on 4th December 1939,

Manchester Regiment was run down by Pacific Steam Navigation Co.'s *Oropesa* (14,118/1920) which had been detached from a North Atlantic convoy to pick up the crew of Harrison's *Chancellor* (4,607/1916), itself sunk in collision with *Athelchief* (7,707/1925). *Manchester Regiment* sank with the loss of nine lives. *[Upper: Peter Newall collection; lower: National Maritime Museum P16575]*

LONDON COMMERCE (top), **ROYAL PRINCE** (middle) and **COLLEGIAN** (bottom)
Furness Shipbuilding Co. Ltd., Haverton Hill-on-Tees; 1923, 7,886gt, 472 feet
Two single-reduction geared turbines by Richardsons, Westgarth and Co. Ltd., Hartlepool.

Launched as *Australiana* and delivered as *London Commerce*, the second of the group had a career which ran closely in parallel with *London Mariner*. Transferred to Prince Line as *Royal Prince* in 1928, she was probably too large for the Far Eastern trade, and entered lay up alongside her sister in 1931 (as seen right). Harrison purchase saw her become *Collegian*, and she alone of their quartet survived the war, although she was sold to BISCo. for scrap in December 1947 and broken up at Milford Haven. Allowing for her five years of idleness, she had given just 19 years' service. *[Top: Peter Newall collection; middle: A. Duncan, courtesy Bill Schell]*

LONDON SHIPPER (top), **BRITISH PRINCE** (middle) and **STATESMAN** (bottom)
Furness Shipbuilding Co. Ltd., Haverton Hill-on-Tees; 1923, 7,939gt, 468 feet

Two single-reduction geared turbines by John Brown and Co. Ltd., Clydebank.

Furness registered the five *London* ships under several company titles, although all were on essentially the same service. Launched as *Nataliana*, *London Shipper* was owned by the Norfolk and North American Steam Ship Co. Ltd. She is seen above at Vancouver on 2nd September 1926.

Renamed *British Prince* in 1928, she went into lay-up alongside her sisters in late 1930. She was helpful in getting her sisters back into service, however, as Harrisons were actually loaned her in early 1935 for a trial voyage. This must have proved satisfactory, as she and her sisters were purchased in May, *British Prince* becoming *Statesman*.

Statesman was a victim of a Focke-Wulf Fw200 Condor, a civil airliner which became a serious threat to Allied shipping when turned into a maritime reconnaissance bomber and flown with determination by Luftwaffe crews of KG40. *Statesman* was bombed on 17th May 1941, north west of Ireland inward bound from New Orleans with general cargo including steel and sailing independently, as did many faster ships. Casualties were fortunately light, 50 of the 51 aboard escaping in the boats and being picked up within a few hours. *[Middle: National Maritime Museum, courtesy Peter Newall; bottom: Zwaenepoel collection, World Ship Photo Library]*

LONDON MERCHANT (above) and
POLITICIAN (below)
Furness Shipbuilding Co. Ltd., Haverton Hill-on-Tees; 1923, 7,896gt, 472 feet
Two single-reduction geared turbines by John Brown and Co. Ltd., Clydebank.
Seen above at Vancouver on 16th August 1926, *London Merchant* (launched as *Canadiana*) was destined to be the most famous - or perhaps infamous - member of the quintet because of her farcical ending. She escaped transfer to Prince Line, but not lay up in the Blackwater where she was first to arrive in April 1930.

In 1935 Harrisons renamed her *Politician*, as which she was to become, under the pseudonym *Cabinet Minister*, the star of a novel and film. On 5th February 1941 she struck rocks off the island of Eriskay in the Outer Hebrides. No enquiry seems to have been carried out, and there is no satisfactory explanation of why a ship manned and maintained to the high standards expected of a major Liverpool shipping company should pile up in this way, although rain, darkness and the dimming of navigation lights were clearly factors. The Barra lifeboat rescued the crew after they made an abortive attempt to get away in the *Politician's* boats.

But it was *Politician's* cargo which included 22,000 cases of whisky that led to her infamy, as the inhabitants not just of Eriskay, but also of Barra, Uist, Skye and Mull came to help themselves. Bumbledom in the shape of H.M. Customs helped the affair become farce, leaving the protection of the cargo in sole charge of one local customs officer, and even at one time attempting to blow up the remainder of the whisky, simply because duty had not been paid on it. This, plus Compton Mackenzie's novel 'Whisky Galore' and a subsequent Ealing comedy, helped ensure the islanders who plundered the ship emerged as heroes.

Politician was actually refloated in September 1941, but had to be beached again when the naval tug involved was called away on what someone considered a more important job. Winter gales broke her back before she could be refloated, although most of the hull was recovered, with only the stern and fifth hold left on the beach.

The lower photograph shows *Politician* leaving Liverpool for Beira on 18th April 1936.

LONDON IMPORTER (above) and **RELIANT** (below)

Furness Shipbuilding Co. Ltd., Haverton Hill-on-Tees; 1923, 7,938gt, 472 feet Two single-reduction geared turbines by John Brown and Co. Ltd., Clydebank.

It is somewhat ironic that the only one of this group of ships to become an official combatant had one of the least adventurous wars, and survived to a ripe old age.

Laid up since June 1931, *London Importer* was sold to the Admiralty in 1933 and became the Royal Fleet Auxiliary *Reliant*. Needing a stores ship, Their Lordships were probably attracted by her large refrigerated capacity.

Initial service was with the Mediterranean fleet, and at Malta in February 1934 she relieved the *Perthshire*, which appeared in *Record* 9, page 42. By 1942 *Reliant* had moved to the Indian Ocean, and was based at Mombasa with occasional visits to Alexandria for refitting. In 1944 she was called home, and at Wallsend was fitted for Far Eastern Service, receiving the luxury of air conditioning and an enhanced outfit of anti-aircraft guns. These probably never fired in anger, however, and following the surrender of Japan *Reliant* was disarmed and made her way home from Colombo to Chatham.

After being laid up in the Gareloch, *Reliant* was transferred to the Ministry of Transport in March 1948 and put up for sale. Buyers were the Malta Cross Steamship Ltd., which - unlike the many latterday companies using Malta as a flag of convenience - seems to have been a genuine Maltese company, under the management of Anthony P.H. Griscti and Son of Valetta who renamed her *Anthony G*. Within a year, however, she was owned in Pakistan by the East and West Steamship Co. as *Firdausa*. She was broken up at Gadani Beach in 1963 at 40 years of age, having given at least twice the service of her four sisters.

The upper photograph was taken at Vancouver on 19th July 1926. *[Lower: Michael Cassar]*

THE PLM COLLIERS 1 TO 10
Roy Fenton

During the First World War several industrial organisations which depended on sea transport to maintain regular supplies of coal faced such disruption in deliveries that they decided to buy their own ships. It was not just enemy action which was responsible for the shortage of ships: governments quickly requisitioned them for use as transports and as fleet colliers, whilst freight rates for available vessels quickly inflated.

In the United Kingdom the companies who supplied London with its gas took the decision to buy their own ships in an effort to guarantee coal supplies and to stabilise shipping costs. In France a major railway company took a similar decision to maintain its supplies of locomotive coal, la Compagnie des Chemins de Fer de Paris et à Lyon à la Mediterranée, PLM. As in the case of the London gas companies, the PLM became so convinced of the benefits of operating its own ships that in post-war years it made a major investment in purpose-built colliers. France had its own supplies of coal, but these were inadequate for its needs, as shown by the great amount of British coal imported both pre-and post-war. In 1916, in addition, many of the coal mines in the north of France were, if not in German-occupied territory, certainly disrupted by the proximity of the Western Front.

Colliers from the USA

When the PLM decided to become a shipowner in 1916 its first problem was finding ships. Shipyard capacity was largely occupied with warship construction and repair, and there were restrictions on the sale of British ships to foreigners, even if they were allies. The latter explains why the French Government had to take the unusual step of establishing its own company under the British flag, the Bay Shipping Co. Ltd. The PLM turned initially to the east coast of the USA and bought three ships which were engaged in the Atlantic coal trade. The intermediary for these purchases was the Oriental Navigation Corporation, New York, who purchased the ships from US owners. The price was high: $762,500 each for ships which had been built for between $300,000 and $462,500. The Oriental Navigation Corporation registered the ships under the Uruguayan flag, probably because US owners were not allowed to sell vessels to belligerents. However, the ultimate destination of the ships was well known; the US shipping press reported that they were being sold to the

An almost-new *Edison Light* ghosts into Boston on 17th December 1912. In 1916 she was to become *PLM 1*, first of the fleet, but went missing later that year. *[Hildebrand collection, courtesy Bill Schell]*

French Government, of which the Oriental Navigation Corporation seems to have been an agency. Its president was Philip C. De Ronde of New Jersey, whose name suggests he was of French descent. The colliers probably made no more than their trans-Atlantic delivery voyage under the Uruguayan flag.

With little imagination the ships were named, or rather numbered, *PLM 1* to *PLM 3*. But although these titles did not disguise the ultimate ownership by the railway, the ships were actually registered under the name of the Société Nationale d'Affretêments. This has been described as the PLM's shipowning arm, and was later to operate another series of colliers bearing its own initials, SNA.

Two further ships were added to the PLM fleet, also built at Ecorse, Michigan on the Great Lakes. They were taken over whilst still building and completed as *PLM 4* and *PLM 5*. The former had been christened *M.E. Harper* but no US name has been discovered for the latter. Although acquired by the Oriental Navigation Corporation, it is not known if they were put under the Uruguayan flag.

Colliers from anywhere

Other acquisitions made at the height of unrestricted submarine warfare in 1917 suggest that, as the USA became involved in the conflict, suitable ships became even more difficult to find. Purchases included one almost new Japanese ship, an older Greek tramp, two elderly British tramps, and a further US East Coast collier which was sold directly to the French. All were larger than the first five ships.

The PLM ships would load coal in British ports - such as those in South Wales or on the north east coast (*PLM 7* was photographed at Blyth) - and sometimes at Dunkirk, all for delivery to Marseilles. The waters around Great Britain were by this stage of the war a happy hunting ground for German submarines, but only one PLM ship is known to have suffered at their hands, the *PLM 4* being torpedoed in December 1917. However, of the ten ships

bought during the First World War, only seven or at most eight were in service at any one time, as in addition to this loss the *PLM 1* went missing in November 1916 and the *PLM 3* sank after a collision a year later. The usual hazards of the sea were made worse in wartime by the extinguishing of lights and re-routing of ships to avoid areas of reported submarine activity. Losses continued after the Armistice, with the *PLM 9* wrecked in December 1918. But like the London gas companies, the French railway had developed a taste for shipowning, and its next step was a bold one of ordering a fleet which included some sophisticated colliers.

The article will conclude in the next issue with the purpose-built colliers from Tees-side yards

FLEET LIST - PART ONE

1. PLM 1 1916
2,549g 1,699n 247.0 x 43.7 x 28.6 feet
T. 3-cyl. by Great Lakes Engineering Works, Ashtabula, Michigan, USA; 274 NHP.
10.1912: Completed by Great Lakes Engineering Works, Ashtabula, Michigan (Yard No. 104) for the Boston Virginia Transportation Co. (W. Harper junior, manager), Boston, USA as EDISON LIGHT.
1914: Manager became C.G. Stoddard.
1916: Sold to Phineas H. Sprague, Portland, Maine, USA (C.H. Sprague and Son Inc., Boston, managers).
1916: Sold to the Oriental Navigation Corporation, New York, USA.
1916: Acquired by Société Nationale d'Affrêtements, Paris and renamed PLM 1
31.10.1916: Left Cardiff for Marseilles with a cargo of coal.
2.11.1916: Sailed from Penzance Roads and went missing.
27.2.1917: Reported to have been torpedoed and sunk in the Atlantic.

Photographs of the first ten PLMs under French ownership have proved elusive, perhaps not surprising in view of their often short wartime careers under PLM names. The only one found so far is *PLM 7*, nestling amongst other colliers at Blyth which include to her left the Norwegian *Hassel* (3,968/1905) and further left Denholm's *Glenpark* (2,133/1918). [George Scott collection]

Although dimensionally identical to *Edison Light*, the *Penobscot* - which became *PLM 2* - was a very different-looking ship, with no cargo gear and a bridge forward of amidships. She is seen above at Boston on 20th April 1913, and on the opposite page after her nine years as *PLM 2* and various other adventures, as *Tristan*, back in US waters some time after 1928 and very considerably rebuilt.

The *Tristan* was photographed by Captain William J. Taylor, regarded as one of the best ship photographers working on the Great Lakes. Employed by the US Lighthouse Service, for many years he captained one of their lighthouse tenders, giving ample opportunity for photography. Incredibly, considering the quality of his work, he used a home-made camera taking 8 x 10 inch film. [Upper: Hildebrand collection, courtesy Bill Schell; right: Captain William J. Taylor, J.N. Bascom collection]

2. PLM 2 1916-1925

O.N. 143986 2,294g 1,669n 247.0 x 43.7 x 28.4 feet
T. 3-cyl. by the Great Lakes Engineering Works, Detroit, Michigan, USA; 291 NHP.
10.6.1911: Launched by the Great Lakes Engineering Works, Ecorse, Michigan, USA (Yard No. 84).
8.1911: Completed for the Harper Transportation Co., Boston, USA as PENOBSCOT.
1915: Owner became the Shawmut Steamship Co., Boston.
1916: Sold to the Oriental Navigation Corporation, New York, USA.
1916: Acquired by Société Nationale d'Affrêtements, Paris and renamed PLM 2.
6.1925: Sold to Mrs. Letitia L. Mackay (Adam B. Mackay, manager), Hamilton, Ontario, but registered in Swansea and renamed LAIRG.
1927: Sold to the Nova Scotia and St. Lawrence Navigation Co., Nova Scotia.
14.9.1927: Seized by US authorities at Pennsylvania when attempting to smuggle liquor under the name BULKO.
23.11.1927: Sold at auction to Charles E. Gremmels, New York. Her UK register was closed on 13.3.1928.
1928: Sold to the Morecraft Transportation Corporation, New York, USA and renamed PENOBSCOT.
1928: Sold to the Hammermill Paper Co., Erie, Pennsylvania, USA and renamed TRISTAN.
1933: Sold to the Buckeye Steamship Co. (J.T. Hutchinson, manager), Cleveland, Ohio, USA.
1941: Sold to Madrigal and Co., Manila, Philippines.
1949: Owners became the Madrigal Shipping Co. Inc., Manila and renamed LEPUS.
20.10.1956: Foundered in position 19.15 north by 126.15 east, about 200 miles east north east of Luzon, during Typhoon Jean whilst on a voyage from Legazpi to Hirohata, Japan with a cargo of scrap iron. 25 of the crew of 36 were lost.

3. PLM 3 1916-1917

2,294g 1,666n 247.0 x 43.7 x 28.4 feet
T. 3-cyl. by the Great Lakes Engineering Works, Detroit, Michigan, USA; 192 NHP.
9.1911: Completed by the Great Lakes Engineering Works, Ecorse, Michigan, USA (Yard No. 86) for the Harper Transportation Co., Boston, USA as F.J. LISMAN.
1915: Owner became the Shawmut Steamship Co., Boston, USA.
7.1916: Sold to the Oriental Navigation Corporation, New York, USA.
1916: Acquired by Société Nationale d'Affrêtements, Paris and renamed PLM 3
19.11.1917: Sank following a collision with the French steamer PSYCHE (2,951/1904) off Ile de Groix whilst on a voyage from Newport to St. Nazaire with a cargo of coal.

4. PLM 4 1916-1917

2,640g 1,325n 253.0 x 43.5 x 25.6 feet
T. 3-cyl. by the Great Lakes Engineering Works, Detroit, Michigan, USA; 284 NHP.
9.1916: Completed by the Great Lakes Engineering Works, Ecorse, Michigan, USA (Yard No. 162) for Société Nationale d'Affrêtements, Paris as PLM 4. She had been building for the Clinchfield Navigation Co., New York, USA. as the M.E. HARPER and was later acquired by the Oriental Navigation Corporation, New York.
27.12.1917: Torpedoed and sunk by the German submarine UC 71 in the English Channel 28 miles north east of Barfleur whilst on a voyage from the Tyne to Havre with a cargo of coal.

5. PLM 5 1917-1925

2,820g 1,508n 253.0 x 43.5 x 25.6 feet

T. 3-cyl. by the Great Lakes Engineering Works, Detroit, Michigan, USA; 284 NHP.

10.1916: Completed by the Great Lakes Engineering Works, Ecorse, Michigan (Yard No. 163) for Société Nationale d'Affrêtements, Paris as PLM 5. She had been building for the Clinchfield Navigation Co., New York, USA and was later taken over by the Oriental Navigation Corporation, New York.

3.1925: Sold to the Polish Government (Naval Department), Warsaw, Poland and renamed WARTA.

1927: Owners became Panstwowe Przedsiebiorstwo 'Zegluga Polska', Gdynia, Poland.

1932: Owners became 'Zegluga Polska' Spolka Akcyjna, Gdynia, Poland.

1935: Sold to Orazio Resini (A. Barabino fu A., managers), Genoa, Italy and registered in Budapest, Hungary.

1935: Sold to B. Burger e 'Finagra' S.A. (B. Burger, managers), Genoa, Italy but registered in Budapest, Hungary and renamed TURUL.

1938: Owners became Société Anonyme Maritime et Commerciale, Geneva, Switzerland (c/o Anglo-Swiss Maritime Co. Ltd., London), but registered in Budapest, Hungary.

1940: Registered in Panama.

19.12.1954: Arrived at Milford Haven to be broken up by T.W. Ward Ltd.

6. PLM 6 1917-1921

O.N. 145468 3,244g 1,951n 305.0 x 43.7 x 27.2 feet

T. 3-cyl. by Osaka Iron Works Ltd., Osaka; 288 NHP, 1,400 IHP, 10 knots..

4.1916: Completed by Osaka Iron Works Ltd., Osaka (Yard No. 869) for K. Hashimoto, Sasebo, Japan as KIFUNEZAN MARU.

1916: Owners became Hashimoto Kisen Gomei Kaisha, Sasebo.

3.1917: Acquired by Société Nationale d'Affrêtements, Paris and renamed PLM 6.

2.11.1921: Registered in the ownership of the Bede Steam Shipping Co. Ltd. (Frew, Elder and Co. Ltd., managers), Newcastle-on-Tyne and renamed BEDEBURN.

7.5.1930: Sold to the Dunelm Shipping Co. Ltd. (Germain, Dixon and Co. Ltd., managers), Newcastle-on-Tyne.

4.7.1930: Renamed AIKLEAF.

9.1.1936: Sold to the Nailsea Steamship Co. Ltd. (E.R. Management Co. Ltd., managers), Cardiff under the Scrap and Build scheme. Resold to Metal Industries Ltd., Rosyth for £4,650.

29.1.1936: Arrived at Rosyth for demolition which began on 12.2.1936.

19.2.1936: Register closed.

The Japanese-built *PLM 6* was sold to Newcastle owners in 1921, becoming *Bedeburn*, as seen here at Cape Town. [R.M. Scott, Ivor Rooke collection]

7. PLM 7 1917-1922

3,189g 2,030n 331.0 x 47.7 x 22.5 feet

T. 3-cyl. by Central Marine Engineering Works, West Hartlepool; 277 NHP.

15.6.1908: Launched by William Gray and Co. Ltd., West Hartlepool (Yard No. 754).

7.1908: Completed for Basilios B. Fameliaris, Syra, Greece as FAMELIARIS.

1915: Sold to N.E. Ambatielos, London and renamed AMBATIELOS under the Greek flag.

1917: Acquired by Société Nationale d'Affrêtements, Paris and renamed PLM 7.

9.1922: Sold to Pithis Brothers and G. Corakis, Chios, Greece and renamed PARTHENON.

1923: Manager became A.J. Pithis.

1928: Manager became D.J. Pithis.

1930: Managers became Pithis Brothers and Co., Alexandria, Egypt.

3.11.1942: Torpedoed and sunk by the German submarine U 442 and/or U 522 in position 53.30 north by 42.15 west whilst on a voyage from Botwood and St. John's, Newfoundland to the Mersey in convoy SC 107. Six of the 27 crew and two gunners were lost.

8. PLM 8 1917-1922

3,289g 1,980n 318.5 x 49.5 x 24.2 feet

T. 3-cyl. by the New York Shipbuilding Corporation, Camden, New Jersey, USA; 318 NHP.

30.11.1915: Completed by the New York Shipbuilding Corporation, Camden, New Jersey (Yard No.164) for the Pocahontas Navigation Co. Inc. (Coastwise Transportation Co., managers), Boston, USA as VIRGINIA.

1915: Sold to the Harby Steamship Co., New York.

1916: Sold to the Gaston, Williams and Wigmore Steamship Corporation, New York, USA.

1917: Acquired by Société Nationale d'Affrêtements, Paris and renamed PLM 8.

26.9.1922: Wrecked off Cape Razo, Portugal whilst on a voyage from Philippeville to Rotterdam with a cargo of coal.

9. PLM 9 1917-1918

O.N. 106829 3,011g 1,939n 312.0 x 42.5 x 20.5 feet

T. 3-cyl. by the North Eastern Marine Engineering Co. Ltd., Wallsend-on-Tyne; 250 NHP, 1,500 IHP, 10 knots.

17.11.1896: Launched by C.S. Swan and Hunter Ltd., Wallsend-on-Tyne (Yard No. 209).

12.1896: Completed.

18.12.1896: Registered in the ownership of the British and Foreign Steamship Co. Ltd. (Rankin, Gilmour and Co., managers), Liverpool as SAINT MARY.

14.4.1906: Sold to Joseph Hoult, Liverpool.

15.5.1906: Renamed BENRATH.

22.2.1907: Owners became the Steam Transport Co. Ltd. (Joseph Hoult, manager), Liverpool.

1912: Sold to Joseph Constant, London.

1914: Sold to S.A. Gerakis and Co., Marseille, France and renamed ANDREAS GERAKIS under the Greek flag. UK register closed on 6.3.1914.

1917: Acquired by Société Nationale d'Affrêtements, Paris and renamed PLM 9.

4.12.1918: Wrecked near Penmarch whilst on a voyage from St. Nazaire to Swansea in ballast.

10. PLM 10 1917-1928
O.N. 109970 3,107g 1,980n 330.1 x 48.5 x 21.6 feet
T. 3-cyl. by Central Marine Engineering Works, West Hartlepool; 280 NHP, 1,300 BHP, 9 knots.
21.6.1898: Launched by William Gray and Co. Ltd., West Hartlepool (Yard No.560).
9.1898: Completed.
8.9.1898: Registered in the ownership of the London and Northern Steamship Co. Ltd. (Pyman Brothers Ltd., managers), London as EASINGWOLD.

12.5.1916: Sold to David P. Barnett, Cardiff.
5.7.1916: Owners became the Italian Export Shipping Co. Ltd. (David P. Barnett, manager), Cardiff.
1917: Acquired by Société Nationale d'Affrêtements, Paris and renamed PLM 10. UK register closed on 1.5.1917.
1928: Sold to G. and T. Mabro, Alexandria, Egypt and renamed ANGELE MABRO.
1936: Owners became T. Mabro.
6.7.1940: Left Bilbao for Cardiff and disappeared.

Last of the wartime acquisitions was the aging British steamer *Easingwold*, which became *PLM 10* in 1917. This photograph in Pyman Brothers' colours shows their trade mark beaked stem, for which they retained a predilection until the 1920s. *[K. O'Donoghue collection]*

SOURCES AND ACKNOWLEDGEMENTS

Photographs are from the collection of John Clarkson unless otherwise credited. We thank all who gave permission for their photographs to be used, and for help in finding photographs we are particularly grateful to David Whiteside and Tony Smith of the World Ship Photo Library; to Ian Farquhar, Bill Laxon, Peter Newall, Ivor Rooke, William Schell, George Scott; to David Hodge and Bob Todd of the National Maritime Museum; Dr. David Jenkins of the National Museums and Galleries of Wales; and other museums and institutions listed.

Research sources have included the Registers of William Schell and Tony Starke, *Lloyd's Register, Lloyd's Confidential Index, Lloyd's War Losses, Mercantile Navy Lists,* and *Marine News.* Use of the facilities of the World Ship Society's Central Record, the Guildhall Library, the Public Record Office and Lloyd's Register of Shipping are gratefully acknowledged. Particular thanks also to William Schell, Tom Adams and John Bartlett for various information, to Heather Fenton for editorial and indexing work, and to Marion Clarkson for accountancy services.

The PLM colliers
Thanks in particular to Bill Schell, who very kindly obtained ships' US registration documents from National Archives, and helped provide photographs of the earlier ships under US ownership. A French railway journal, *Connaissance du Rail,* issue No. 125 of June 1991 carried a brief article on the later P.L.M. ships which inspired the author to research them further. Docteur Paul Bois of Toulon was generous both with supplying photographs of the later PLMs and reading through the text. Thanks also to Jay Bascom of Toronto for supplying the superb print of *Tristan* and for biographical details of the photographer Captain Taylor. Earlier versions of this article appeared in *Nautibel* 28 and 29, and in *Tees Packet.*

Spanish veterans
Thanks to Hubert Hall, Louis Loughran, Christy MacHale, John Naylon and Richard Osborne for background information. As well as the general sources referred to above, the following were consulted:
Welsh Blockade Runners in the Spanish Civil War by Heaton PM, P.M. Heaton, Pontypool, 1985
Steam Collier Fleets MacRae JA and Waine CV, Waine Research Publications, Albrighton, 1990.
Elder Dempster Fleet History 1852-1985, Cowden JE and Duffy JOC, Mallett & Bell Publications, Coltishall, 1986
Marina Mercante en el País Vasco (1960-1990), Servicio Central de Publicaciones del Gobierno Vasco, Vitorio-Gasteiz, 1996 (we are grateful to

Louis Loughran for pointing out this source).
'Naval actions of the Spanish Civil War 1936-39.' Osborne R. In: *Warships Supplement: Proceedings of Naval Meetings* Osborne R. ed. World Ship Society, Kendal, 1989. Thanks to Dr. Osborne for providing this source, which helps to explain the naval events of this bloody and complex conflict.

From tanker to ferry
The original version of this article, by Frank Heine, appeared in the German-language magazine *FERRIES- Das Fährschiffahrtsmagazin* in 1997. With Frank's permission, Roland Whaite used Internet translation software to produce a rough draft which he then updated and rewrote with additional research whilst sourcing mostly different photographs for *Record.*

The Welly Boot
Ship's histories in the captions are from *Blue Star* by O'Donoghue K. and Atkinson T. World Ship Society, Kendal, 1985, and sources listed above. Photographs and details of the arrival of *Southland Star* and *Wellington Star* in Bangladesh for breaking up appeared in an article by Michael Pryce in *Marine News* 1995, **49**, 28-9.

Their own devices
Histories of the ships illustrated were drawn from sources listed above and from:
Empire Tugs, Harvey WJ and Turrell K. World Ship Society, Kendal, 1988.
Ships in Focus: Anchor and Brocklebank Lines. Clarkson J and Fenton R. J. and M Clarkson, Preston, 1994.
Ships in Focus: Burns and Laird Campbell C and Fenton R. Ships in Focus Publications, Preston, 1999.
Deutsche Reedereien Band 6, Detlefsen GU, Verlag Gert Uwe Detlefsen, Bad Segeberg, 1997.

Two funnel postscript - Glenogle of 1882
Glen Line to the Orient Harnack EP, Glen Line, London, 1970.
Merchant Fleets: Glen and Shire Lines Haws, D. Duncan Haws, Hereford, 1991
The China Bird: The History of Captain Killick and One Hundred Years of Sail and Steam MacGregor DR, Chatto & Windus, London, 1961
Merseyside Maritime Archives, Glen MSS, OA113, Steamer Earnings, 1871-98.
Returns of Ships Hired..., House of Commons Papers, 1886, Vol.41.
Closed Register, Public Record Office, BT110/784.

SPANISH VETERANS

For some years after the Second World War, Spain had a wonderful collection of veteran steamers, due partly to economic backwardness, and possibly as a result of the protectionist policies of General Franco's fascist regime. The following photographs are from the collections of Captain Hubert Hall, who suggested the idea and supplied basic career details, and of John Clarkson. A number of other contributors had an input including Christy MacHale, John Naylon and Louis Loughran. The ships are arranged in chronological order of build.

SIMANCAS (above)
J.L. Thompson and Sons, Sunderland; 1892, 3,028gt, 322 feet
T. 3-cyl. by J. Dickinson, Sunderland.
Helped by an attractive arboreal background, the external condition of *Simancas* does not suggest she is the oldest ship here, 73 years of age when captured in April 1965 by a photographer based in Avilés. Clearly, there has been some rebuilding of her superstructure.

    Simancas was built for the Rowland and Marwood's Steamship Co. Ltd. of Whitby as *Blue Cross*. This was an odd choice of name, and is intriguing as at the time she was built the owners used a *red* cross on their flag and funnel, changing to a *blue* cross only in 1934, following complaints that it would lead to confusion with ships carrying the markings of the Red Cross.

    Blue Cross was sold in 1913 to become the *Sineus* belonging to a G.W. Schröder of Riga and Petrograd, who was presumably adjudged a German as, after the First World War, the ship was taken over by the UK, although quickly returned

to the owner, who sold her on to Spain in 1921. Spanish names were *Suárez No.1*, *Alfonso Senra*, and from 1939 right up until her demolition at Avilés in October 1967, *Simancas*. Owners of *Simancas* were Gumersindo Junquera S.A. of Gijón, whose crossed-flags marking can still be seen on funnels and houseflag, the latter unusual in having a flag on a flag. *[Estudio Novel, Avilés, courtesy Hubert Hall]*

SAC SANTANDER (opposite top and middle)
Short Brothers, Sunderland; 1895, 2,555gt, 304 feet
T. 3-cyl. by Blair and Co. Ltd., Stockton-on-Tees.
To all those who prefer underway shots, with hardly the distraction of a horizon, we offer no apology for the upper photograph opposite, taken in Livorno on 30th March 1951, bustling with life, cargo, and steam. *SAC Santander* has probably brought a grain cargo from one of the South American ports and it is being discharged into the port's characteristic lighters using the ship's gear and the muscles of Italian stevedores and lightermen.

    SAC Santander was one of two early completions at Sunderland for King Line Ltd., launched into the Wear as *King David*; the other being *King Edgar* (2,552/1896). In ten years she was in Spanish hands and, as this feature will show, these hands tended to keep their ships until a ripe old age. First *Acuario*, she became *Teresa Pamies* in 1911, and *SAC 9* in 1932. Although they suggest an association with sherry, the initials SAC actually came from the then owner, Soc. Anón. Cros of Barcelona. In 1948 they changed their name, rather radically, to Transportes, Aduanas y Consignaciones

S.A., although this did not affect their funnel colours nor their naming scheme: indeed *SAC 9* was renamed *SAC Santander* in 1950. The middle photograph opposite shows the 68-year old veteran awaiting attention from the breakers at Barcelona on 9th April 1963. *[Both: John Clarkson collection]*

UROLA (opposite bottom)
Russell and Co., Port Glasgow; 1898, 3,482gt, 339 feet
T. 3-cyl. by Rankin and Blackmore, Greenock.
The *Urola* is a reminder that shipbuilder Russell and Co. was not only associated with series production of big sailing ships (see *Beechbank* in *Record* 14) but, until 1918 when merged into Lithgows Ltd., built many steamers, two of which turn up in this feature.

    Urola was built for Sigval Bergesen as *Storfond*, and after a creditable 21 years of Norwegian ownership was sold to Spain to become *Mercedes*. But her Spanish career was only just beginning, and after receiving the name shown here in 1923, she managed another 32 years. Not that these weren't adventurous: during the Spanish Civil War *Urola* was bombed and sunk at Valencia, although raised in June 1939 and returned to service. She is seen at Montevideo on 25th May 1947 in the colours of her owner since 1942, Compañía Naviera Espanola S.A. of Madrid: black funnel with a six-pointed white star on a blue band.

    Life had one more big adventure for the old ship; whilst on a voyage with coal from La Coruna to Barcelona on 24th March 1955 she was in collision in fog with the Soviet *Vtoraya Pyatiletka* (5757/1919) off Portugal, and sank. *[John Clarkson collection]*

APOLO (above)

Napier and Miller Ltd., Glasgow; 1900, 4,320g, 375 feet

T. 3-cyl. by David Rowan and Co., Glasgow.
Spain's neutrality in both the twentieth century's major wars helps explain the longevity of some of its ships, although the Spanish Civil War inevitably brought its own casualties. *Apolo* escaped its dangers through being laid up from September 1937 to 1939. Indeed, in a charmed 64-year life she had just one name and one owner: Compañía Anónima Marítima Unión of Bilbao (for whom she was built and in whose colours *Apolo* is seen here) which changed its name to Naviera Bilbaina S.A. in 1952. *Apolo* was broken up in her home port in 1964. *[Hubert Hall collection]*

ALBAREDA (below)

Russell and Co., Port Glasgow; 1903, 3,925, 345 feet

T. 3-cyl. by Rankin and Blackmore, Greenock.
Those looking for a family resemblance between this Russell product and the *Urola*

on the previous page will be disappointed: *Albareda* has a long bridge deck, and even details like cross trees are different, although in the course of long careers either or both ships could well have been modified.

Albareda was completed as *Provan* for a long-forgotten Newcastle owner, J. Lockie and his Ceres Steam Shipping Co. Ltd. Within a year she was bought by a far better-known Tyneside outfit, Knott's Prince Line, who renamed her *British Prince*. She was acquired by Spain in 1922, and remained under the red and gold flag for well over 40 years. Names were *Guadiaro, Udondo, Gante, Albareda* (as seen here in the ownership of José de Navas Escuder of Bilbao) and lastly *SAC Coruña*. Astute observers will note that that the funnel has an 'N' on it for Navas. This is the patronimic surname, Escuder being the less important matronimic surname. The ship was broken up in Spain during 1965. *[John Clarkson collection]*

MINA CANTIQUÍN (opposite top)

Compañiá Euskalduna de Const. y Rep. de

Buques, Bilbao; 1905, 1,235gt, 226 feet
T. 3-cyl. by Central Marine Engineering Works, Hartlepool.
A variety of Basque names were bestowed on this Bilbao-built and registered steamer for her first couple of decades. Built as *Getso* for what is probably the best-known Basque shipowner, Compañía Naviera Sota y Aznar, she became *Arza Mendi* for the same owners in 1917, then *Ybai-Patxo, Iturri-Patxo* and later *Rola* for other Bilbao owners. When photographed at Málaga in 1966 she was *Mina Cantiquín* in the colours of Naviera del Nalón S.A. of Gijón, with whom she ended her days, being broken up in 1972.

With the exception of the last, all the names this ship carried were Basque. The De La Sota family, part owners, had backed the losing Republican side during the Spanish Civil War, and had to continue their shipowning in exile across the French border in Biarritz. Louis Loughran tells how in 1970 he was surprised to see the *Artiba* at Liverpool wearing as a stem

jack the Ikurriña, the flag of the Basques. *Artiba* (7,709/1958, ex-*Baron Kinnaird*) had the funnel marking of the Artagan Shipping Co. Ltd., a Liberian-flag subsidiary of Ramon de la Sota Junior, who at this period had placed all his ships under flags of convenience. The Basque Government issued a decree in 1937 that the Ikurriña must be flown by all ships controlled, managed or manned by Basques. For many years during the Franco regime, when persecution of the Basques was at its height, the flying or display of the Basque flag was illegal in Spain. Louis was told by Ramon de la Sota Junior that he insisted that his captains fly the Ikurriña when in port, except in Spain. During the 1980s, the use of the Basque flag was legalised, and it can now be seen flying over most of the buildings of any consequence in the Basque provinces. *[Hubert Hall collection]*

CARLOS TARTIERE (below)
Short Brothers Ltd., Sunderland; 1905,1,587gt, 259 feet
T. 3-cyl. by Blair and Co. Ltd., Stockton-on-Tees.
Several ships in this feature came into Spanish ownership as a result of the Civil War. This Sunderland-built steamer had impeccable British credentials, built as *Cairnnevis* for the Cairn Line of Steamships Ltd. of Newcastle-on-Tyne, then in 1919 going to Christian Salvesen as *Tolsta*. The Leith owner sold her to Estonians as *Juss* in 1937, and it was under this name that she was captured by the Nationalist auxiliary cruiser *Mallorca* in the Straits of Gibraltar on 22nd January 1938. Condemned as a prize, she joined the Spanish Government-owned fleet as *Sevilla* and later *Castillo Gibralfaro*.

The Nationalists captured more prizes during the Civil War than would be expected from their limited naval power.

During the attempted rightwing coup d'etat which began the war in July 1936, the generals made the mistake of ignoring the Spanish Navy, assuming it would remain neutral. This was not the case, however, as the crews had mainly Republican sympathies. Nevertheless, the gradually increasing numbers of warships which came into Nationalist hands were handled with considerably more daring than those which remained loyal to the Republican Government, and in particular were able to successfully blockade Mediterranean ports, with some help from their better-equipped Italian allies.

Carlos Tartiere is seen leaving Gijón in 1957, her freshly-painted hull suggesting that she had recently been renamed by her owner since 1952, Compañía de Naviera Vasco-Asturiana of Avilés. After one further change of owner, but not of name, she was broken up in Spain in 1974. *[Hubert Hall collection]*

MUNISA (above)
Charles Connell and Co. Ltd., Glasgow;
1907, 4,937gt, 400 feet
T. 3-cyl. by David Rowan and Co. Ltd.,
Glasgow.
Not all the Spanish freighters surviving into post-war years still looked original, and *Munisa* has undergone serious attempts at modernisation. Comparison of the excellent trials shot as *Den of Ruthven* in David Burrell's 'Den Line' shows that a split superstructure has given way to a composite one with a hold ahead of it on the bridge deck. Further British owners followed C. Barrie and Sons, and she carried the names *Wyncote* and *Kintyre* until sold to Greece in 1929 to become *Polymnia*, becoming the French *Sydney* in 1937.

On 17th December 1937 *Sydney* was captured by a Nationalist auxiliary cruiser in the Straits of Gibraltar, and entered service for the Nationalists as *Coruña*. A series of Government and private owners followed, as she became *Castillo Simancas*, *Jarama*, *Rivademar* and finally in 1963 *Munisa* for Naviera Forestal Africana S.A. She is almost unique in this feature in meeting her end due to marine hazard, as on 28th April 1972 she was beached after hitting a rock off Greenville, Liberia and became a total loss. She was on a voyage from Duala to Santander with logs. *[Foto Reguera, Pasajes, courtesy Hubert Hall collection]*

VIERA Y CLAVIJO (below)
Caledon Shipbuilding and Engineering Co.
Ltd., Dundee; 1912, 862g, 210 feet
T. 3-cyl. by Caledon Shipbuilding and
Engineering Co. Ltd., Dundee
By way of change from general cargo ships, *Viera y Clavijo* has accommodation for some 176 passenger and ran interisland services in the Canaries. In 1930 original owners Compañía de Vapores Correos Interinsulares Canarios - a name which needs almost no translation - gave way to Compañía Trasmediterránea, also of Las Palmas.

When retired in 1978 after a very creditable 66 years' service, the old steamer was sold to Dutch owners, and temporarily became *Jomar*, although she soon reverted to *Viera y Clavijo*. Attempts were made to preserve her but, possibly because she had no connection with her adopted country, even the Dutch who have a superb record in preservation could not save her, and she does not appear in recent editions of the *International Register of Historic Ships*. Information on her current status or fate would be appreciated. *[Hubert Hall collection]*

RÍA DE VIGO (above)
Irvine's Shipbuilding and Dry Dock Co. Ltd., West Hartlepool; 1912, 3,847gt, 350 feet
T. 3-cyl. Richardsons, Westgarth and Co. Ltd., Hartlepool.
Photographed in Montevideo on 30th November 1946, *Ría de Vigo* was another ship which the fortunes of war put into Spanish ownership. By then - 1943 - she was already an old lady, but had several decades of further service in her.

She had at least five British owners, being built as *Newfield* for J.J. and C.M. Forster of Newcastle-on-Tyne, becoming the *Apsleyhall* of the West Hartlepool Steam Navigation Co. in 1918, and two years later the Cardiff-owned *Cymric Queen*. *Record* 16 featured some of the ships built for E. and R. Management Ltd., and this is one of the old steamers with which they commenced shipowning, bought in 1932 and renamed *Nailsea Brook*. In 1935 a final British owner gave her the lovely name *Boscombe Chine*, but sold her to Germany in 1937. As *Helios* she was in Lisbon in September 1939, but was subsequently moved to Spanish waters. These were presumably judged friendlier to the Nazi cause, or perhaps just gave better prospects of a sale, as she turns up in 1943 under the ownership of Empresa Nacional 'Elcano', the state-owned Spanish line, in whose colours she is seen. As *Ría de Vigo* she returned to private hands in 1947, retaining her name until broken up at Santander in August 1966. *[John Clarkson collection]*

BARTOLO (below)
J. Priestman and Co., Sunderland; 1918, 3,118, 331 feet
T. 3-cyl. by George Clark Ltd., Sunderland.
Not a post-Second World War veteran (in fact, she was a victim of it), but it was hard to resist this First World War standard ship, photographed by John McRoberts on 26th January 1933.

The Shipping Controller named her *War Zephyr*, but quickly sold her to W.H. Vernall and Co. of London who renamed her *Algorta*, only to pass her on to a branch of Strick Line. She became *Bartolo* of Compañía Naviera Bachi in 1925. Manager was Hijos de Astigarraga of Bilbao: note the 'A' on the funnel.

On 6th March 1943 HM Submarine *Taurus* sank the neutral *Bartolo* off Sète towards the end of a voyage from Savona to Marseilles. *Bartolo* is described as 'blacklisted', presumably because she was suspected of carrying cargo for Vichy France. It is a matter of record that it took six British torpedoes to sink her. *[John Clarkson collection]*

OPHIR (above)
Echevarrieta y Larrinaga, Cádiz, 1919, 549gt, 164 feet
T. 3-cyl. by Alexander Brothers, Barcelona.
With the catwalk over the deep well between forecastle and bridge, and limited deck space, *Ophir* looks so much like a tanker that it is surprising that she was built as a dry cargo vessel, and converted in 1927. After conversion owners were Compañía Arrendataria del Monopolio de Petroleos S.A., a state-owned company which certainly deserves abbreviating to CAMPSA. *Ophir* lived through the Civil War, but was captured by Nationalists at Malaga in February 1937. She seems to have returned to her owners and enjoyed no further notoriety until broken up in Spain early in 1967. *[Roy Fenton collection]*

ALINE (below)
John Lewis and Sons Ltd., Aberdeen; 1920, 1,452gt, 235 feet
T. 3-cyl. by John Lewis and Sons Ltd., Aberdeen
Watched by onlookers, the steamer *Aline* ghosts into a Spanish port - probably Gijón - at least forty years after she was built during the period of great optimism which immediately followed the First World War. She was ordered for one of the many Cardiff companies that dreamed of sharing in the riches that were apparently being earned by shipowners but, almost invariably, these dreams turned to nightmares as the high price of the newbuildings had to be repaid from plummeting freight rates.

As *Madge Llewellyn* she was of a size suitable for exporting steam coal to ports around the Bay of Biscay and Mediterranean. Her original owners were one of several shipping companies in which coal owner Sir David R. Llewellyn sank his fortune, the Llewellyn Shipping Co. Ltd. In 1925 its four ships passed to the Federated Shipping Co. Ltd. without change of name, suggesting that Llewellyn was still the main shareholder. In 1928 the four were sold again, this time to the Cardigan Shipping Co. Ltd. and once more without change of name.

In 1938 *Madge Llewellyn* became the *Dellwyn* of Claude Angel, another Welshman with ships under a variety of different ownerships. By now, with the Spanish Civil War at its bloody height, British owners who had experienced almost two decades of gloomy rates could make excellent profits, albeit at high risk to

their ships and crews, by trading to ports held by the Republicans but under blockade by Franco's Nationalists. Angel's ships were frequently reported in such ports, and *Dellwyn* was soon one of those which paid the price of blockade running. With another Angel ship, she was unloading coal in the port of Gandía in July 1938 when attacked by Nationalist aircraft, and after five days of bombing and machine gunning, was sunk by a direct hit on 27th July. Fortunately, her crew were ashore and were not injured.

The port of Gandía was captured in March 1939, and in May the *Dellwyn* was raised and repaired for return to service for the Spanish Government as *Castillo Motesa*, subsequently being transferred to the state-owned Empresa Nacional Elcano. She passed back into private hands in 1961, to become *Aline* as shown here, owned in Gijón by Angel Riva Suardíaz. She was broken up in her home port in 1970. *[Hubert Hall collection]*

EL CONDADO (middle)
William Hamilton and Co. Ltd., Port Glasgow; 1920, 3,472gt, 331 feet
T. 3-cyl. by Dunlop, Bremner and Co. Ltd., Port Glasgow.
Alejandro Navajas of Bilbao took delivery of *El Condado* from the Clyde in 1920, and his family seems to have run her right up until mid-1976 when she was broken up in Spain. The only change recorded was registration under Compañía General de Navegación, managed by Navajas, in 1922. *[Hubert Hall collection]*

VIZCAYA (bottom)
Ateliers et Chantiers de la Gironde, Harfleur; 1923, 4,579, 377 feet
T. 3-cyl. by Schneider et Compagnie, Havre.
As a change from the mostly British-built tramps, here is a French-built one. *Vizcaya* was originally *Joseph Magne*, becoming *Bizkaya* around 1930. From 1936 she was in Italian ownership as *Padova*. In 1939 she returned to her previous Spanish owners as *Bizkaya*, suggesting that Italian ownership might have been in response to the Civil War. With suppression of all things Basque by General Franco, the ship adopted the less Basque-sounding spelling *Vizcaya* and retained this under the ownership of Naviera Bilbaina S.A. until broken up in 1964. *[Hubert Hall collection]*

FROM TANKER TO FERRY Part 1
Frank Heine and Roland Whaite

The shifting patterns of trade in the shipping industry have occasionally given rise to quite extensive conversion projects. Passenger ships and ferries have become cable layers or livestock carriers, lightships have re-emerged as sail training vessels, and changing values in the bulk commodity markets have led to vessels being stretched or shortened whilst switching between dry and liquid cargoes.

One of the more unlikely schemes to come to fruition saw a number of mostly Scandinavian tankers converted in the 1960s and 1970s by Greek and Italian shipyards to serve the emerging ferry and ro-ro trades in the Mediterranean. It could not have been obvious to contemplate stripping out tanks, pipework and pumps to allow the insertion of vehicle decks whilst simultaneously cutting the hull openings for the access ramps, but a number of factors had come together to make this a commercial proposition.

The tanker market had seen a rapid expansion in vessel size from the early post-war years, when there had been little change in dimensions from their pre-war counterparts, to the early 1960s by which time orders were commonplace for vessels exceeding 100,000 tons deadweight. Some redundancy fed down through the market, resulting in the ready availability of modern hulls and machinery at much cheaper prices than a newbuilding.

At the same time, the numbers of individual travellers using private passenger cars had begun to rise so that demand for drive-on drive-off ferries in replacement of traditional crane loading had reached the Mediterranean basin. However, most liner services were operated by pure passenger ships or by limited conversions from such conventional vessels, and since the northern European car ferry market was in its own early stage of development, there were no examples available for sale to migrate southwards.

Notably, at the start of the decade, Hellenic Mediterranean Lines launched their newbuilding *Egnatia* (6,185/1960) whilst Adriatica provided the *Appia* (8,017/1961), each equipped with a stern ramp as entry to a garage deck holding 120 cars, for the cross-Adriatic services between Italy and Greece, but few other companies could afford to follow this lead.

During the period from 1963 to 1976, eleven tankers were purchased for conversion, five to become passenger car ferries in Greek hands, with a further two as freight-only ro-ros (although one was to remain unconverted) whilst Italian yards transformed four more for commercial lorry traffic, mostly destined to trade well beyond the Mediterranean shores.

The first purchases
In 1963, Constantinos S. Efthymiadis operated just two 1944-vintage landing craft-type ferries but was about to embark on an expansion programme which was to see Efthymiadis Lines own 15 cruise ships and passenger ferries at its peak in the early 1970s.

This Greek shipowner was the first to see the possibility that a tanker conversion would provide a faster and cheaper creation of a ferry than a newbuilding could offer. In May 1963, he purchased the 12-year old *Maria Gorthon* from Stig Gorthon of Helsingborg. At nearly 500 feet, this product of the Kockums yard in Malmo represented a substantially larger starting point than any other ferry then working in the Mediterranean. The *Maria Gorthon* was renamed *Phaistos* and registered in Piraeus, before being moved in the spring of 1964 to a local Perama shipyard for the rebuilding to commence. At about that time, a second Swedish-owned tanker was acquired, the slightly larger *Soya-Margareta* of Olof Wallenius. On arrival in Piraeus, she became the *Minos* and by November 1964 she was also lying at Perama. Meanwhile the conversion of the *Phaistos* gathered speed.

Maria Gorthon, the first tanker to be converted to a ferry. *[World Ship Photo Library collection]*

Phaistos - the first conversion

By the time the *Phaistos* emerged for the summer season of 1965, she had undergone a substantial transformation. Painted white overall, the basic hull form was still recognisable, but an extended superstructure connected the bridge and the aft accommodation blocks and carried eight additional lifeboats on the uppermost deck to allow for a passenger certificate of 670.

Although the oil tanks were all removed, the car deck did not extend fully into the forepart of the ship and necessarily terminated forward of the machinery spaces, being served by side ports in front of the bridge on both starboard and port sides. Vehicles could also be loaded on the foredeck using the original derrick to give a possible total capacity of 200 cars. The garage deck had sufficient headroom that 60 trucks could alternatively be carried.

Despite these modifications, the gross tonnage was re-measured at 8,134 tons, lower than in the tanker configuration because the garage was not regarded as an enclosed space within the calculations then current. As indicated by her name (*Phaistos* is a Minoan palace site in the south of Crete, sometimes rendered as *Festos* in English) she commenced service on a regular overnight run from Piraeus to Crete.

The original MAN diesel driving a single screw was retained, giving a service speed of around 13 knots, but *Phaistos* was underpowered and, in the absence of a bow thruster, proved a difficult ship to manoeuvre in the confines of Piraeus Grand Harbour or the Souda Bay terminal near Chania in Crete; and she often required tug assistance in berthing during her next ten years of activity.

Phaistos in service at Piraeus (above) and laid up (below) amongst other Efthymiadis vessels. *[Above: Michael Cassar; below: Antonio Scrimali]*

Minos - the second conversion

Later in 1965, the former *Soya-Margareta* also entered the Cretan run, but with the main port of Iraklion as the island terminal. *Minos* had undergone a similar conversion as *Phaistos*, with much the same layout and an identical certificate for 670 passengers. Her slightly larger dimensions gave a capacity of 220 cars or 70 trucks, and her single diesel was considerably more powerful to give a service speed of just under 15 knots.

The *Minos* was mentioned in the world headlines following the loss of the Greek passenger ship *Heraklion* on 8th December 1966 near the Aegean island of Falconera. A less substantial conversion than the *Minos*, the *Heraklion* (11,300/1949) was the former Bibby motorship *Leicestershire*, similarly equipped with side ports and a garage by Typaldos Lines for their own Piraeus to Crete service. The subsequent inquiry established that a lorry had broken loose in a storm and smashed open the starboard loading door allowing water to enter so quickly that the vessel capsized and sank within ten minutes of the first distress call. A total of 217 lives were lost, and there were only 47 survivors amongst passengers and crew, most of whom were found clinging to rocks off the island. These survivors were taken on board the *Minos* in the immediate aftermath of the rescue.

The *Minos* and the *Phaistos* continued on their respective Cretan runs into the 1970s, the only significant change occurring in 1971 when the passenger certificate for both vessels was increased to 1,000.

Soya-Margareta (above) before her 1965 conversion and as *Minos* at Piraeus on 14th April 1977 (below). *[Above: W.H. Brown, World Ship Photo Library collection; below: Ambrose Greenway]*

Soya-Birgitta. [Fotoflite incorporating Skyfotos]

Two more purchases from Sweden

With both the initial vessels in service, Constantinos Efthymiadis went back in October 1965 to Olof Wallenius in Stockholm for the *Soya-Birgitta*. Yet again built by Kockums, she had almost identical dimensions as the *Maria Gorthon* but had been completed two years later. Arriving in Piraeus as the *Sophia*, she was soon joined by the *Heleanna*.

The *Heleanna* had a slightly different pedigree, emerging from the Gotaverken yard as the *Munkedal* in 1953. At nearly 550 feet long, she was the largest of the four tankers so far acquired by Efthymiadis, who paid around £200,000 to obtain the vessel.

The conversion of *Sophia* followed similar lines to that of *Phaistos* and *Minos*, but the hull was built up in the forward section allowing a nearly continuous passenger deck to extend below the weather deck. Vehicles could be transferred to the open deck space forward using an elevator lift from the garage space, and the eight new lifeboats were hung in more modern gravity davits.

Again the *Sophia* was certificated for 670 passengers and 200 cars, with the passengers being accommodated in a mix of two berth, four berth and eight berth cabins and lounges equipped with airline-type reclining chairs. Since she was destined for the Adriatic, and in particular for the Patras to Ancona route where two nights would be spent at sea on every trip, *Sophia* was not only provided with a restaurant, bar and cafe, but also with a swimming pool and a duty-free shop. Again, her original MAN diesel provided a service speed of around 14 knots.

One year after the *Sophia* entered service, the *Heleanna* replaced her on the Patras to Ancona run enabling the *Sophia* to shift to Piraeus and partner the *Minos* to provide a daily sailing to and from Iraklion. In 1967, the *Heleanna* was one of the largest car ferries in the world and bigger than most ferries operating in the North Sea or the Baltic. She initially boasted a slightly lower passenger count (620) than the *Sophia* whilst carrying 20 more cars.

A well-patronised *Sophia* at Corfu on 12th September 1975. [Ambrose Greenway]

Munkedal (above) and as converted to *Heleanna* at Valetta in 1968 (below). *[Above: World Ship Photo LIbrary, below: Michael Caesar]*

A new Greek company takes a tanker

One result of the *Heraklion* disaster mentioned above was the creation of a company funded by public subscription on the island of Crete and encouraged by church patriarchs. The Cretan Maritime Company ANEK (Anonymos Naftiliaki Etereia Kritis A.E.) was formed in 1967 and acquired as their first ship the Dutch-built tanker *Wirakel* from Suomen Tankkilaiva O/Y of Helsinki. She had been built in Rotterdam by the P. Smit yard and had much the same dimensions as the *Maria Gorthon* and the *Soya-Birgitta*.

Named after a former King of Crete, the *Kydon* arrived in Piraeus on 23rd August 1968 and immediately moved to the Perama yards. Her rebuilding was to be much more substantial than any of the other vessels, and she was not to enter service until 1970.

Garage deck access was not only from large side ports positioned under the bridge, but also from smaller side ports aft, although the latter could only handle private cars. Even with headroom of around 14 feet for trucks, a near full-length cabin deck was accommodated within the hull. Two further passenger decks between the bridge and after

Wirakel. [Fotoflite incorporating Skyfotos]

superstructure allowed cabins to be provided over three decks and the lower of these decks extended forward of the remodelled bridge front.

A new radar mast was placed behind the bridge, the after goalpost mast retained and the funnel given a streamlined casing with a distinctive fin. Extra liferafts were stored either side of the funnel allowing the passenger capacity to be set at 860.

Registered in Chania, the *Kydon* was to prove the longest serving of any of the tanker conversions, staying as part of the rapidly enlarging ANEK fleet until the end of the 1988 season, mostly on the route from Piraeus to Souda, a few miles from her theoretical homeport across the Akrotiri peninsula.

Views of *Kydon* at Piraeus, in 1982 (top) and in September 1987 (middle), and in her final guise as *City of Taranto*. [Top: Peter Newall; middle: Roland Whaite; bottom: Antonio Scrimali]

Two more for Efthymiadis

Before the *Kydon* came into service, Efthymiadis Lines acquired two more tankers from Scandinavia, but this time both came from Norwegian owners. The *Thorsholm* had been operated by Thor Dahl for 15 years since her construction at Uddevalla, and was the biggest vessel yet to be acquired, whilst the Framnaes-built *Fermita* had already had two previous names (*Emerald* and *Morgedal*) before her most recent service with Uglands of Grimstad.

Although respectively named *Efthycosta I* and *Efthycosta II*, both vessels continued in the tanker trades for a time until on 8th April 1970 the latter vessel was in collision with the British coastal tanker *Esso Ipswich* (1,103/1960) off Penarth. Both vessels sustained significant damage, and some of the crude oil that *Efthycosta II* was transporting from Milford Haven to Cardiff drifted down the Bristol Channel towards Barry Island, contaminating local beaches.

After initial repair at Cardiff, the decision was taken to proceed with the ro-ro conversion, and *Efthycosta II* left South Wales on 28th April, arriving at Perama nine days later. Unlike the previous conversions, the superstructure remained relatively unchanged, but the amidships house below the bridge was remodelled to provide a through deck for the carriage of trucks; an internal ramp connected this weather deck to the main car deck where advantage was taken of the capacious hull to ensure headroom of about 14 feet, as in the *Kydon*. Access was through a side door and ramp forward of the amidships structure on each side of the ship.

When this conversion was completed later in 1970, the blue-hulled *Efthycosta II* was the largest short-distance freight ferry in the world, and the first to be completed with two vehicle decks. With the Gotaverken diesel giving a service speed of 13.5 knots, *Efthycosta II* could complete a round trip between Piraeus and Iraklion every two days.

Three stages in a career: Emerald as a tanker (top), as Efthycosta II during conversion to a ferry (middle), and in service at Rhodes in 1973 (bottom). [Top: Fotoflite incorporating Skyfotos; middle: Antonio Scrimali; bottom: Ambrose Greenway]

Efthycosta I was never converted as intended, but was laid up at Perama in 1974 and broken up four years later.

Loss of the Heleanna

During the summer of 1971, all four Efthymiadis passenger vessels were certificated for raised numbers towards the one thousand mark. The authorisation for *Heleanna* to carry 945 came through on 26th August, only two days before a fire broke out in the galley at 5.30am in the morning off the Italian coast whilst sailing from Patras to Ancona.

With the fire getting rapidly out of control, the order to abandon ship was given some two hours later, but there is little doubt that this was far too late for an orderly evacuation under the conditions, with some lifeboats already burnt, and others not fully occupied whilst several were overfilled. A day-long rescue operation ensued and once the final count was established, 25 lives had been lost, and upwards of 150 people injured; it was also clear that the vessel had been carrying almost one hundred more passengers than even the expanded certificate allowed.

The subsequent investigations by the Piraeus Public Prosecutor led to the trial, in 1974, of six men, ranging from the ship's cook through the first and second engineers to the first mate and the master of the *Heleanna*, along with the owner, Constantinos Efthymiadis, on manslaughter charges. The commission of inquiry had found that known defects in a paraffin stove had not been eliminated, that the vessel was carrying more passengers than certificated, that some of the fire-fighting equipment was not functioning, that life saving drill was rarely enacted so that the crew did not know their duties, and on the occasion of the fire that general alarm warnings were issued to passengers too late, and the order to go to evacuation stations had only been made once the situation had been critical for some time.

All the indicted crew members were given imprisonment and forbidden to serve again on Greek ships, and the owner also received a period of detention. Efthymiadis Lines were faced with substantial claims for damages, and were to decline rapidly into bankruptcy. The findings from the *Heleanna* disaster also contributed to revisions of the SOLAS code in 1974.

The *Heleanna* did not sink but was towed into the outer harbour of Brindisi, where the fire was extinguished on the afternoon of 30th August. Most of the vessel was gutted although the sprinkler systems had prevented some cars from being burnt. With the police investigations lasting for some months, the hulk was towed firstly to Perama and then to La Spezia before being sold on to Toulon breakers in the spring of 1974. The hull was cut down to form an unpowered barge.

The decline of Efthymiadis Lines

In the aftermath of the loss of the *Heleanna*, the remaining three passenger conversions stayed on the Cretan runs, whilst the Patras to Ancona route was served by the conventional passenger ship *Olympia* (10,945/1953), formerly the *Pierre Loti* of Messageries Maritimes. This vessel was converted into the car ferry *Patra* in the winter of 1973/74, with the Italian terminal moving to Brindisi.

In the spring of 1974, the *Minos* was sold to the newly-emerged Minoikai Grammai A.N.E., later better known as Minoan Shipping Lines S.A., a private company established in Iraklion and using a funnel marking incorporating a figure from one of the frescoes in the Minoan palace of Knossos. With the name unchanged as the first vessel for the company, *Minos* made its initial commercial sailing from Iraklion to Piraeus on 5th July 1974.

Both the *Phaistos* and the *Sophia* were laid up from 1975. On the 17th May 1976 it was realised that the *Sophia* was taking in water, and she was hurriedly towed clear of navigation channels and beached in the vicinity of Keratsini. Listing some 60 degrees to port, the *Sophia* remained a constant part of the local scene until breaking began in the spring of 1986. At least one fire broke out during the process, but the last remnants had disappeared by the end of that year.

By the end of 1976, Efthymiadis Lines were formally declared bankrupt, and the *Phaistos* plus the two *Efthycostas* were available at auction. Initially, there were no buyers for the *Phaistos* and the *Efthycosta I*; the latter had not traded since 1973 and was scrapped in the summer of 1978.

Although ANEK and Minoan Lines were direct competitors, they agreed each was to take a 50 per cent share in *Efthycosta II* to provide a community service particularly for trucks carrying dangerous goods. Renamed *Zakros* (again the name of a Minoan palace) and given a plain white funnel whilst retaining the dark blue hull, she commenced running from Iraklion to Piraeus in 1977 and was sometimes to be seen transporting army vehicles in this service.

Initially, very little interest was shown in *Phaistos*, but in 1980 a new company named Greek Ferry Lines acquired the vessel from the creditor banks, and announced plans to start a Brindisi to Patras service for the following year. The *Phaistos* received the name *Grecia*, and limited modifications were undertaken. The Greek maritime authorities then took a hand, and as a result of their surveys refused to authorise any use as a passenger ship. Initially left lying at Ambelaki, the *Grecia* finally moved to the Eleusis scrapyards in 1983.

The three survivors

As the 1970s moved into the next decade, *Kydon*, *Minos* and *Zakros* provided a regular and reliable part of the service from Piraeus to Crete, with the passenger vessels often lying over in Piraeus during the day after an early morning arrival from the island and scheduled to return sometime after 6pm; *Zakros* had a certificate allowing 40 berthed drivers to accompany their vehicles and operated sailings as demand arose.

Minos suffered one incident towards the end of 1982, when she was found to be leaking water whilst in harbour at Piraeus, but swift action saw her towed into dry dock and quickly repaired. However, her days were by then numbered as single screw ferries were due to be phased out as part of improved safety considerations. Removed from service at the start of 1984, she was towed away in May to breakers in Santander.

Zakros only lasted into the following year, being withdrawn in the summer and arriving under tow at Split at the end of September 1985. However, ANEK were reluctant to dispose of *Kydon* immediately, so it was not until the introduction of the former Japanese *Aptera* (7,058/1973) at the beginning of 1988 that she was replaced on the Chania service.

During that summer, *Kydon* was tried on a new Iraklion to Thessaloniki circuit, but was placed on the sales list in the autumn. In the spring of 1989, despite by then being 36 years old, *Kydon* was acquired by an investment company associated with Greek shipowner Antonis Lelekis. Renamed *City of Taranto* and Maltese-registered, she commenced a short-lived service linking the southern Italian port of Taranto with Patras. This was suspended at the end of August, and she then operated for a few months on behalf of the Libyan Government between Valletta and Tripoli.

The final incarnation saw the *City of Taranto* in a static role at Chalkis as an accommodation ship for Polish workers in the Avlis shipyard, also owned by Tony Lelekis. The Lelekis empire fell upon hard times during the 90s, and this last survivor of the tanker-to-ferry conversions arrived at Aliaga in Turkey during August 1998.

Record 18 will continue the story with the Italian conversions of tankers to ferries.

Sophia half submerged in Perama Bay, August 1977. *[Antonio Scrimali]*

Conversions in Greek yards

1. PHAISTOS/GRECIA 1963-1983

Greek O.N. 2210 (LR: 5413006) 8,134g 6021n 151.29 x 18.95 metres

M.A.N. oil engine 7-cyl. 2SCDA by Kockums M/V A/B, Malmo; 4,500 BHP, 13.5knots

11.1951: Completed by Kockums M/V A/B, Malmo (Yard No. 318) for Rederi A/B Gylfe (Stig Gorthon, manager), Helsingborg as MARIA GORTHON (8,864g 5,075n 13,235dwt).

5.1963: Sold to Constantinos S. Efthymiadis, Piraeus and renamed PHAISTOS.

1964-1965: Converted to a passenger ro-ro in Perama.

1975: Laid up by Efthymiadis Lines near Salamis Island.

1976-1980: In hands of creditor banks.

1980: Sold to Greek Ferry Lines, Piraeus and renamed GRECIA; returned to lay-up after refit stopped.

1983: Scrapped Eleusis.

2. MINOS 1964-1984

Greek O.N. 3 (LR: 5336143) 9,517g 6,577n 162.57 x 19.23 metres

M.A.N. oil engine 6-cyl. 2SCDA by Kockums M/V A/B, Malmo; 6,000 BHP, 14.75 knots.

5.1952: Completed by Kockums M/V A/B, Malmo (Yard No. 343) for Rederi A/B Wallstar (Olof Wallenius, manager), Stockholm as SOYA-MARGARETA (10,731g 6,263n 16,075dwt).

1964: Sold to Constantinos S. Efthymiadis, Piraeus and renamed MINOS.

1964-1965: Converted to a passenger ro-ro at Perama.

1974: Sold to Minoikai Grammai Anonymos Naftiliaki Etereia, Iraklion.

5.1984: Towed to breakers at Santander.

3. SOPHIA 1965-1976

Greek O.N. 2627 (LR: 5336129) 8,945g 5,827n 151.29 x 18.95 metres

M.A.N. oil engine 6-cyl. 2SCSA by Kockums M/V A/B, Malmo; 5,400 BHP, 14 knots.

9.1953: Completed by Kockums M/V A/B, Malmo (Yard No. 361) for Rederi A/B Walltank (Olof Wallenius, manager), Stockholm as SOYA-BIRGITTA (9,005g 5,123n 12,965dwt).

10.1965: Sold to Constantinos S. Efthymiadis, Piraeus and renamed SOPHIA.

1965-1966: Converted to a passenger ro-ro at Perama.

1975: Laid up by Efthymiadis Lines near Salamis Island.

17.5.1976: Taking in water, beached at Keratsini with 60 degree list and abandoned.

1986: Broken up in situ.

4. HELEANNA 1966-1971

Greek O.N. 2838 (LR: 5243748) 11,674g 7,759n 167.30 x 20.27 metres

Oil engine 9-cyl. 2SCSA by A/B Gotaverken, Gothenburg; 6,800 BHP, 14.75 knots.

1.1954: Completed by A/B Gotaverken, Gothenburg (Yard No 679) for Rederi A/B Monacus (Tord Selden, manager), Kungsbacka as MUNKEDAL (11,232g 6,538n 17,610dwt).

1966: Sold to Constantinos S. Efthymiadis, Piraeus and renamed HELEANNA.

1966-1967: Converted to passenger ro-ro at Perama.

28.8.1971: Vessel caught fire 12 miles from Torre Canne (Italian Adriatic Coast). Order to abandon ship given in position 48.58 north by 17.35 east 1,102 lives saved, 25 lost.

29.8.1971: Towed towards Brindisi, tow broke, aground at San Cataldo.

30.8.1971: Refloated, towed into Brindisi outer harbour, fire extinguished.

1972: Wreck towed to Perama.

16.2 1974: Wreck arrived in tow at La Spezia for breaking by Ditta Lotti.

1974: Resold to Toulon breakers and hull cut down to an unpowered barge.

5. KYDON/CITY OF TARANTO 1968-1998

Greek O.N. 8 (LR: 5392173) 10,714g 7,610n 153.93 x 19.97 metres

Oil engine 6-cyl. 2SCSA by N.V. Maschinefabriek & Scheepswerft P. Smits Junior, Rotterdam; 5,530 BHP, 14.25 knots.

6.1953: Completed by N.V. Maschinefabriek & Scheepswerf P. Smits Junior, Rotterdam (Yard No. 605) for Suomen Tankkilaiva O/Y, Helsingfors as WIRAKEL (10,016g 5,541n 14,510dwt).

8.1968: Sold to Anonymos Naftiliaki Etereia Kritis (A.N.E.K.), Chania as KYDON.

1968-1970: Converted to passenger ro-ro at Perama.

1989: Sold to Jo-Dim Investment Ltd, Valletta and renamed CITY OF TARANTO.

1990: Laid up at Chalkis with Tony Travel and Agency Ltd. as managers.

10.8.1998: Arrived under tow at Aliaga for breaking.

15.8.1998: Demolition commenced by Iska Metal A.S.

6. EFTHYCOSTA I 1969-1978

Greek O.N. 3695 (LR: 5360261) 173.01 x 21.32 metres

Gotaverken oil engine 8-cyl. 2SCSA by Uddevallavarvet A/B, Uddevalla; 7,500 BHP, 14 knots.

1954: Completed by Uddevallavarvet A/B, Uddevalla (Yard No. 132) for A/S Ornen (A/S Thor Dahl, manager), Sandefjord as THORSHOLM (12,423g 7,020n 18,840dwt).

1969: Sold to Constantinos S. Efthymiadis, Piraeus and renamed EFTHYCOSTA I.

1.4.1974: Laid up in Perama (intended conversion not commenced).

1978: Demolition commenced by Prodromos Sariktzis & Co, Perama.

7. EFTHYCOSTA II/ZAKROS 1969-1985

Greek O.N. 3698 (LR: 5241647) 9,957g 5,696n 156.98 x 19.56 metres

Oil engine 8-cyl. 2SCSA by A/B Gotaverken, Gothenburg; 6,000 BHP, 13.5 knots.

1953: Completed by A/S Framnaes M/V, Sandefjord (Yard No. 147) for F. Tenvig & Co. A/S (Rederi A/S Willy Oppens, manager), Oslo as EMERALD (9,957g 5,696n 15,934dwt).

1962: Renamed MORGEDAL and management assumed by Simonsen & Astrup.

1964: Sold to A/S Ugland's Rederi, Grimstad and renamed FERMITA.

1969: Sold to Constantinos S. Efthymiadis, Piraeus and renamed EFTHYCOSTA II.

8.4.1970: In collision with ESSO IPSWICH (1,163/1960) off Penarth.

7.5.1970: Arrived Perama for conversion to ro-ro.

1977: Sold to 50:50 partnership between Anonymos Naftiliaki Etereia Kritis (A.N.E.K.) and Minoan Lines Shipping S.A., registration retained in Piraeus, and renamed ZAKROS.

14.8.1985: Sold to Eckhardt & Co. Marine and delivered at Piraeus for breaking.

30.9.1985: Redelivered to Brodospas at Split for demolition.

Top: *Minos* at Iraklion on 1st August 1976 in Minoan Lines livery. *[Jim McFaul]*
Middle: *Kydon* at Piraeus on 7th June 1980. *[Roland Whaite]*
Opposite and bottom: *Zakros*. *[Opposite: Jim McFaul, Piraeus Roads, 1st July 1979; bottom: Louis Bosschaart]*

THE WELLY BOOT
Captain A.W. Kinghorn

Affectionately nicknamed the 'Welly Boot' by those who sailed in her, the longest-lived *Wellington Star* was the second ship of that name, built in 1952, and broken up in Kaohsiung, Taiwan in 1979.

Her sadly shortlived predecessor was built during those momentous years 1939-40, by Harland and Wolff, Belfast, with her twin sister *Auckland Star*. Following the highly successful *Imperial Star* class of a few years earlier (featured in *Record* 9), the two new sisters were slightly longer - 535.5 feet as opposed to the 524.2/530 feet of the earlier ships. Outwardly, the difference lay in the forward pair of sampson posts which gave the new vessels a fourth derrick for handling cargo at No.1 hatch. The older ships had a third, centre derrick, heeled to the foot of the mast.

But both she and her sister *Auckland Star* were torpedoed by German submarines, fortunately without loss of life, in the North Atlantic, on 16th June and 28th July 1940, respectively. Both liners were homeward bound from Australia with full cargoes of refrigerated and general produce. The loss of the company's two newest and finest vessels so early in the war was a bitter taste of things to come; 29 Blue Star ships were lost before victory was finally won.

Postwar rebuilding

The postwar rebuilding programme set out to provide ships which would maintain and develop the company's prominent place in the prewar cargo liner trades - from Britain and Europe to South Africa, Australia, New Zealand, the west coast of North America and the east coast of South America. The prewar trade with China was put on hold in view of the turbulent political and economic situation prevailing there as a result of the civil war between the Kuomintang and the Communists.

After the four new turbine-driven River Plate cargo passenger liners *Argentina Star, Brasil Star, Uruguay Star* and *Paraguay Star* of the 1946-48 programme (see next spread), and the six-hatch motor vessels *Imperial Star* and *Melbourne Star* built 1947 as war loss replacements for the first *Auckland Star* and *Wellington Star*, a new class of seven-hatch liners was built. Gross tonnages were around 12,000 on a length of 555.2 feet, beam of 72.7 feet, depth 37.1 feet. To compare performance and running costs, steam against diesel, the new *Tasmania Star* and *Auckland Star* were given PAMETRADA-designed steam turbines driving single screws while *Adelaide Star* and *Wellington Star* had twin-screw six-cylinder Doxfords.

Wellington Star, photographed on 27th November 1969 (below), and opposite two of her near-sisters, the turbine-driven *Tasmania Star* (top and middle) and the twin screw motor vessel *Adelaide Star*, the latter seen on 22nd October 1961.

In terms of longevity, there was little to set the turbine and motor ships apart. Both the Cammell Laird-built *Tasmania Star* (11,950/1950) and the John Brown-built *Adelaide Star* were sold to breakers in Taiwan and South Korea respectively within months of each other in 1975, achieving a creditable 25 years' service. The slightly younger diesel-driven *Wellington Star* was sold in 1976, but conversion to a livestock carrier and Panama registration extending her working life until 1979. *[All: Ian Farquhar]*

Blue Star's post-war cargo-passenger quartet were impressive ships, but the accommodation for over fifty passengers gave them a somewhat hunch-backed appearance which even the large Blue Star funnel did little to ameliorate. All four were built and engined by Cammell Laird and Co. Ltd. at Birkenhead, *Argentina Star* (10,716/1947) being the first delivered. Seen above on 17th July 1971, she was still in immaculate external condition despite being little more than a year away from the scrapyard. In 1972 she was sold to a Japanese company who quickly resold her to Taiwan breakers, who took delivery of her in October.

The four ships were delivered with black hulls, but by the time colour photography was widespread they had been given Blue Star's trademark grey hulls with blue boot topping. Below is *Brasil Star* (10,716/1947) on a surprisingly bright River Thames on 11th November 1968. Sold as part of the same deal as *Argentina Star,* she too arrived at Taiwan for demolition in October 1972. Work was completed in January 1973. *[World Ship Photo Library George Gould collection 9317 and 13236]*

Like many immediately post-war Blue Star vessels, the passenger ships gave their whole lives to the company, partly no doubt because by the 1970s turbine-driven ships were becoming expensive to run and their secondhand value was low. *Uruguay Star* (10,732/1947) is pictured above on 16th April 1971 again on the Thames. She arrived at Taiwan for demolition in August 1972.

The last of the quartet built, *Paraguay Star* (10,722/1948) was the first to go. In August 1969 she was discharging in London's Royal Docks when fire broke out in her engine room. Damage was extensive, and given her age and the decline of the passenger business, she was declared a constructive total loss. Decisions were taken quickly, and barely a month after the fire *Paraguay Star* arrived in tow in Hamburg to be broken up by Eckhardt & Co. GmbH. *[World Ship Photo Library George Gould collection 16036 and Les Ring collection]*

The trade

Launched at John Brown's, Clydebank yard on 7th May 1952 by Miss Margaret Vestey, the *Wellington Star* was the third ship of the 'Big Four' to complete and promptly took her place in the booming trade with Australia and New Zealand, occasionally calling at South Africa outward bound. A voyage to New Zealand was made out and home through the Panama Canal with calls at Willemstad in Curacao, or Cristobal in the Canal Zone for bunkers - a typical loading being at London Royal Docks for Suva and Lautoka in Fiji, Auckland, Bluff, Lyttelton, Napier, New Plymouth and Wellington; loading under the meat loaders at Bluff or Timaru, topping up in the deeper water of Port Chalmers. Homeward voyages may have included a brief call at Pitcairn to pick up the islanders' mail, and the first European call was usually Dunkirk, with bales of wool, much of which had been carried as deck cargo: tarpaulin-covered and securely stowed on the hatch tops, clear of any sea coming aboard during the long haul home. A round voyage took about five months.

The weather round New Zealand can be horrendous, the South Pacific rarely lives up to its name for long and not for nothing has the North Atlantic been called the Cruel Sea - ships making these long voyages year after year, deep laden, driving along at seventeen knots, had to be staunchly built and well maintained. There was little room for error. A single 'greeny' coming aboard could do untold damage. Main and all auxiliary engines had to be constantly maintained at the highest efficiency.

The heart of any ship is her electricity generators (or alternators), without which her main and refrigeration machinery could not operate. All 26 cargo derricks with their wire runners and topping lifts, their manila and wire rope guys and preventers, their blocks, hooks and shackles, and their electrical winches - all had to be maintained in perfect condition. To carry out this work the 'Welly Boot' had a total complement, when new, of 68 men, all British. In command was the master, usually a senior and highly experienced captain - deck officers comprised the radio officer, four mates and two cadets. The chief engineer officer was responsible for all things mechanical and there were two seconds, two thirds, two fourths, numerous junior engineers, first and second refrigeration engineers, first and second electrical officers, a full crew of petty officers and ratings, purser/chief steward with his second and assistants, bedroom steward, chief and second cooks, baker and butcher, galley boys and pantry boys. Twelve passengers were comfortably accommodated under the bridge in four single and four double cabins, each with own facilities - as bathroom with bath, washbasin and toilet were styled. The full-length bath's huge brass taps issued a choice of either salt or fresh water, as salt water baths were considered good for rheumatism. A doctor was not mandatory in a ship with less than one hundred souls onboard, but there was in those days no shortage of doctors wishing to take advantage of the free passage provided (actually, the doctor signed on at one shilling per month wages).

The *Wellington Star* and her sisters, with the fine vessels of Federal Line and the New Zealand Shipping Company, Port Line and Shaw Savill, maintained this trade with almost clockwork reliability until the container ships began to make inroads during the nineteen seventies. She was my last ship as second mate before being promoted to chief officer of another ship in 1960, I was her chief officer - the mate - for three voyages between 1969 and 1971 and she was my last ship as chief officer before promotion to master. I had stood by her four-month refit at Smith's Dock, North Shields during 1961, during which she was 'reefer enhanced'.

'Reefer enhancement'

Previously uninsulated general cargo spaces at hatches No.1 and No.6 were to be converted to carry reefer cargo. This interesting job, much of which was undertaken by various subcontractors, included laying afromosia hardwood planking over slabs of cork insulation on the various 'tween decks, insulating and cladding the ship's

Rough weather for *Wellington Star* in the North Atlantic, January 1970. *[Author]*

sides and bulkheads with cork, fibreglass and timber - and installing additional refrigeration machinery. The work also involved drydocking and undocking. All four wooden lifeboats were lowered into the water and thoroughly examined by the Tyne senior Board of Trade surveyor armed with his little hammer and jacknife. This gentleman also examined candidates for their masters' and mates' certificates of competency oral examinations – not a man to trifle with! A Lloyd's Register (engineer) surveyor was also in attendance, as were the company's own superintendents from time to time - though, after making the big decisions, they preferred to leave most of the work supervision to the resident chief engineer and myself, with those other officers who were also standing by.

The first voyage I made in her included a call at Pitcairn Island, that rocky, two miles by one mile outpost almost midway across the South Pacific between Panama and Auckland. My wife accompanied me and we both appreciated this first chance to meet the descendants of the *Bounty* mutineers, for whom we took a consignment of provisions - such homely mail-ordered items as sacks of flour, a refrigerator, cartons of chocolate and bags of soap powder. Arriving half a mile off Adamstown, that tiny settlement where ships usually stopped, the sea was too rough for the longboats to come alongside. Tom Christian, Pitcairn's radio operator, therefore directed us to lay off the Western end of the island, where our cadets lowered cases, cartons, bags, bales and boxes down into the longboats which soon ranged alongside. The island's magistrate, Purvis Young, handed payment for these items to the captain, although they had, by kind arrangement, been carried out freight free. We left laden with fresh fruit, woven baskets and handmade wooden curios, strangely moved by the Pitcairn songs of farewell, 'Sweet bye and bye' and 'Goodbye' sung from the boats as they pulled away back to their island home. And so to Wellington.

New cargoes

Next voyage was different in that in New Zealand we loaded a full cargo of varied refrigerated and general produce for the east coast of the USA and Canada, with empty containers from Montreal to Liverpool. This, we realised, was paving the way for the box boats which have maintained the service ever since.

A six-month voyage, from London back to London, it had included unloading calls at Suva and Lautoka, before completing discharge at Wellington and Bluff. Most of the frozen cargo to be loaded this trip was cartoned beef but we

also took the first ever consignment of fresh, chilled kiwi fruit to the United States. Also, a consignment of frozen ice cream in cartons, which to us smacked strongly of 'coals to Newcastle' until - in Charleston, South Carolina, the ice cream's destination - we learned that this would be used in the manufacture of processed foods. US law forbade the import of butter but there existed no regulations prohibiting the import of ice cream. Carrying temperature was critical - neither too high nor too low - with zero degrees of tolerance. This - we found in Charleston when a happy importer came down to accept it - was his third attempt to ship ice cream from New Zealand. (Two previous shipments, neither carried by Blue Star, had been ruined by fluctuations in carrying temperature.) These two special cargoes were, of course, carried in separate lockers, with which the ship was well provided, off the hatch square in the numerous 'tween decks.

Loading was at New Plymouth, Napier, Lyttelton and Auckland - at which port nearly all hands went down with a particularly virulent form of influenza. The chief electrical officer died of it. At one stage critical in the loading (as the shippers' naturally wanted to cram as much cargo into the ship as possible) only the third mate and I were on deck able to carry out our duties. As well as making continuous rounds of the holds being loaded, each morning we climbed over the ship's side down a rope pilot ladder to measure the distance between the loadline engraved on the ship's side and the actual water line - from which a simple calculation gave us the weight of cargo we could still load; 75 tons weight to the inch.

At Napier we loaded mostly carton beef which came down from the freezing works in covered lorries. One hot sunny morning one of the lorries broke down on the road to the port with the result that the cartons were eventually loaded onboard glistening with moisture, instead of frozen dry. As we knew these wet cartons would congeal together into a solid frozen chunk long before we reached America, we protested to the shippers. As the meat had left the freezer works in good condition the shippers were disinclined to heed our protest, until we pointed out that although the meat itself would indeed be delivered frozen hard, torn and ragged cartons caused by them bonding together in the stow would not be acceptable - packaging is very important! The shipper's offer of a letter of indemnity was declined by us (the captain and me) as letters of indemnity carry no value in a claim against damaged cargo. So, after several days of argument, the offending lorry load of meat - about ten tons - was

Wellington Star at Wellington in November 1969 (left) and at Napier (right). [Both: author]

discharged from the ship and replaced. We had to be very careful that only cargo in perfect condition was loaded, otherwise the ship would get the blame when it was delivered in less than perfect condition - and be billed accordingly. This applied to all cargo loaded, refrigerated and general, so it will be seen that on a seven hatch ship such as the *Wellington Star* loading at all hatches simultaneously, the mates, cadets and refrigeration engineers had to be on the ball all the time.

Eventually our cargo was all aboard, including bales of wool on the hatch tops, and - down to our marks - we sailed for Panama. The US authorities had insisted on all hatches being sealed upon completion of loading, seals not to be broken until we arrived at destination. We were not allowed to deviate to another port unless in dire distress. Crossing the South Pacific, near Pitcairn Island, Captain Stubbings received a radio message to embark a man off one of the RFA ships cruising in the vicinity of the current round of French atomic bomb tests, and take him to Panama - the whole evolution being shrouded in secrecy. We knew not who he was, nor whither he was bound - fortunately we had a spare passenger cabin.

First US port was Charleston (ice cream and meat) followed by Norfolk, Philadephia, New York, transiting the Cape Cod Canal to Boston, and Montreal, unloading in each port, to the expressed satisfaction of the consignees who were unaccustomed to seeing their cargo delivered in such a large 'limejuice' ship! In Montreal we loaded standard sized 20-foot empty containers for London.

Later life
Expecting fog crossing the Grand Banks of Newfoundland, we were pleasantly surprised to have fine, clear, sunny weather all the way over to the English Channel - with only a moderate swell and no gales. My deck crew had worked and behaved so well throughout the voyage that, unusually,

I had no hesitation in asking them all back for the next trip.

The 'Welly Boot' continued in the UK/Europe to Australasia service until 1976 when, having served her owners well for 24 years, she was sold to the Greek-owned Broad Bay Shipping Co. Ltd. who had her converted in Singapore to carry live sheep as well as frozen mutton - the quick and the dead. Renamed *Hawkes Bay*, her funnel painted green and Panama replacing London as the port of registry on her shapely stern, she ran thus until 1979, when she was broken up at Kaohsiung.

Wellington Star (3) began life as the *New Zealand Star* in 1967 at Bremer Vulkan Schiffbau, Vegesack, a double-Stülcken cargo liner. She and her twin sister *Southland Star* were the last two conventional cargo liners Blue Star built and it was a sign of the times that ten years later, in 1977, both returned to their German builders for conversion to fully cellular container ships - as which they lost none of their old elegant appearance.

The old 'Welly Boot' had recently gone to the Greeks and a new *New Zealand Star* container ship was under construction at Haverton Hill-on-Tees - so it was fitting that the present *New Zealand Star* should be renamed in her new containerised role, *Wellington Star*, to be engaged on the transPacific service between New Zealand and the west coast of North America, manned, by this time, largely with Fijians. As such she lasted until 1993 when she took the long lonely road to that latterday scrapyard, up the beach near Chittagong, Bangladesh.

The second *Wellington Star* and her three big sisters were in many ways the four most successful ships Blue Star Line ever built. The right ships at the right time, they were appreciated as such by those who owned them, shipped cargo in them, supplied them with victuals, dunnage, stores and all the necessities, and not least by those who sailed in them. They helped provide a shipping infrastructure sadly missing in Britain today.

In 1967, Blue Star took delivery of two twin-Stülcken equipped ships, *Southland Star* (11,300/1967) seen opposite and *New Zealand Star* (11,300/1967) (this page upper, taken 15th July 1973). The name *Wellington Star* was used for the third and last time when the latter went back to her builders on the Weser in 1977 to be reconstructed as a container ship (this page lower). With Blue Star's tradition of getting long usage out of their ships, both conversions lasted well, although from 1988 they were registered in Fiji in the ownership of Pacific Coast Shipping Co (Bermuda) Ltd. This concern is listed as a subsidiary of Lion Shipping Ltd., Hong Kong, but management by Blue Star Ship Management Ltd., with no change of name or funnel colours, strongly suggests that Blue Star still had a financial interest. Both *Southland Star* and *Wellington Star* were broken up in 1993 on Fouzderhat Beach, Chittagong. [*Top: Ian Farquhar, Bottom: Peter Stacey*]

THEIR OWN DEVICES
J. L. Loughran

Flags and flag-like objects are amongst the oldest human artifacts, having been in use since the dawn of civilisation. Over time considerable custom and tradition has accrued as to how they are used and what they contain; some aspects, such as heraldic flags and arms, and the codes of signal flags, are closely regulated; while in others, including houseflags, shipowners have literally been left to their own devices. The same applies to funnel markings, which became important even in the early days of steam, and at the present time have in practice replaced the houseflag for the majority of shipping companies. Although houseflags and funnel markings are in many respects a kind of trade mark, it surprised me to discover that there was no official register or record of them. A couple of Scandinavian countries have made half-hearted attempts to regulate these markings, but nowhere else in the world has even tried. This freedom, while permitting duplication - remarkably few among houseflags as it happens - has resulted in a very wide range of designs and symbols, many of which have interesting significance, or a story behind them, which might escape the casual observer. This article explores a random collection of these.

To the observer, the device on the markings of Seacon Ltd. (1) of London is not readily comprehensible. Established in 1975 as Freight Express Seacon Ltd. by an amalgamation of Sea and Continental Waterways Ltd. and Freight Express Ltd., the markings were adopted about 1978, before the present company title, which dates from 1984. They represent the hull of a vessel under the eaves of the company's covered steel berth at its West Ferry Terminal on the Thames, the first of its kind in the United Kingdom. In business as operators of a considerable number of short sea traders, mainly chartered vessels of the sea/river type, many variants of their basic funnel colours are to be seen, which is not unusual with chartered vessels.

The rather comical fish within a circle of yellow rope on the markings of Helmut Bastian (2) of Bremen may attract attention, but in fact it reveals something of the personal history of this owner. The insignia is from the

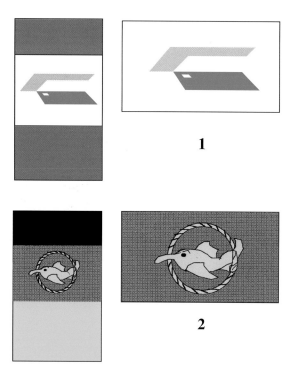

1

2

shoulder patch of the one-man detonation speed boats and submarines of the German navy which Bastian had commanded in the final year of the Second World War. Bastian went into shipowning in 1948, at first in the traditional short sea trades of timber and general cargo. He later expanded into the archetypal geared container ships, of which German yards have built so many, and in 1985 even had two specialised newsprint carriers built for charter to Abitibi Paper Co. However, the company ceased trading in 1989.

Charlotte Bastian (998/1956) was Helmut Bastian's sixth ship, delivered by Heinrich Brand Schiffswerft at Oldenburg. After a respectable 16 years' trading, she was sold in 1972 and put under the Panama flag as *Yolimar.* On 21st February 1976, she left Puerto Cortes in Honduras with 1,200 tons of timber but never arrived at her intended destination, the Venezuelan port of Guamache. She is believed to have sunk about 29th February off Tortuga Island, where wreckage and a boat was found. *[George Gould collection, World Ship Photo Library 14253]*

Often, some symbol in a funnel or flag will have reference to an aspect of a company's history. One example is the houseflag of the Matson Navigation Co. Inc. (3) of San Francisco. The Matson family first became shipowners in 1882, with schooners in the inter-islands trade in Hawaii. In 1901 they bought their first steamship, and formed the Matson Navigation Co. The seven stars on the houseflag are said to stand for the seven original ships owned by them, so it would be interesting to learn what the flag looked like in the process of building up this seven-strong fleet. The funnel top was originally black, but it was changed to blue some time in the early 1930s. The houseflag, though, has been unchanged and, as far as I can tell, is probably the oldest houseflag of a United States company still in existence.

The device on flag and funnel sometimes refers to the trade in which the shipowner is engaged. Sometimes it is difficult, if not impossible, to decipher what a particular device is meant to represent; this seems to be increasingly the case with the products of modern design consultants! A device which combines both these qualities was that on the flag and funnel of London Tugs Ltd. (5) which was established in October 1968 by the merger of Ship Towage Ltd. (4) and W.H.J. Alexander Ltd., to monopolise all ship handling towage on the Thames. Ship Towage had itself been a management merger in 1950 of three of the principal ship handling companies: William Watkins Ltd., Gamecock Tugs Ltd., and the Elliott Steam Tug Co. Ltd.; and in 1965 they adopted a single set of markings. The funnel combined the Elliott flag with bands of Watkins red and Gamecock blue, differing in the same proportion as they contributed assets to the new partnership. Interestingly, the actual houseflag differed from that depicted on the funnel, the cross being changed to embody the Gamecock blue. When London Tugs came into being, this blue disappeared from the funnel bands, replaced by the Alexander red between narrow white bands, and the swallowtailed houseflag became rectangular, while the Elliott flag on the funnel remained unchanged. At the centre of the flag was depicted the device which has eluded identification by almost everyone whom I have asked about it. It is in fact two towing hooks on a V-wire. An appropriate, if not very readily apparent reference to the owner's activities also preserved the most distinctive of the original partners' emblems. Not

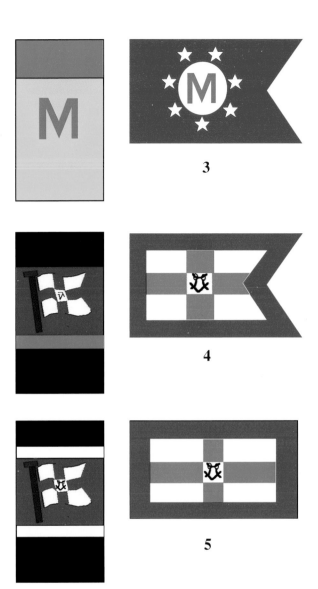

3

4

5

Napia (261/1943) was, like most tugs built during the Second World War, an Empire, *Empire Jester* of the 'Modified Warrior' class. Built at Goole, her engines had to come all the way round from Paisley. William Watkins Ltd. bought and renamed the tug in 1946, and she ended her British career as seen in this 1970 photograph in the ownership of London Tugs Ltd. with funnel (5). Retired from the Thames in 1971, she spent a further 15 years as *Tolmiros* at Piraeus, in which port she was broken up in 1986. [*World Ship Photo Library 22512*]

for long, however. In January 1975 London Tugs was taken over by the Alexandra Towing Co. Ltd., and the Alexandra markings replaced it.

In 1914 Fredrik and Abraham Odfjell (6) formed a shipping company in Bergen, adopting their initial as the device on their flag and funnel, a common enough pattern at the time. Their first ship was named *Birk* (= birch), and set the naming style for subsequent ships until long after their own company had ceased. In 1938 the company was reorganised by the three Odfjell brothers who controlled it at that time. It became Rederiet Odfjell A/S (7) and instead of the single O there was one for each of the brothers, the three circles being interwtined to indicate their partnership. A point worth noting is that each circle is slightly thicker at the point where it intersects another, thus symbolising the strength given by the partnership. The brothers added a *Bow* prefix to the tree names of their ships and increasingly diverted to tankers, eventually operating one of the largest fleets of parcel tankers. As their fleet expanded, different classes of tanker were named after things other than trees, such as birds, though the tree names still remain. In 1978, Abraham and Johan Odvar Odfjell left the company and formed J.O. Odfjell A/S (8), also known as JO Tankers. The original markings of this company showed the company's full initials, but in 1988 this was altered to a logo of the J and O of JO Tankers (9). Possibly because of the departure of the two partners, and almost certainly as a reference to it, Rederiet Odfjell changed its funnel mark in 1980 from the three linked circles to a red chain link on a white funnel. In 1985 there was a reorganisation of all its subsidiary companies into A/S Storli (10) which was controlled by Bernt Daniel Odfjell and in turn managed Rederiet Odfjell. The chain link funnel mark was retained, and shortly after this the field of the houseflag was altered to white to match it.

There are many stories of merchantmen running foul of authority because of the houseflag they were flying: the origin of the 'Paget patch' on the flag of Money Wigram, and later the Federal Line, is too well known to bear repetition here; and the encounter between HMS *Dryad* and Captain Dobson of the *Dotterel* in 1882 which resulted in the blue star being added to the flag of the Cork Steamship Co. is very similar. The boot was on the other foot, however, when the International Code of Signals was being compiled. At first, there were no flags for vowels in this code, the reason given being that 'by introducing them, every objectionable word of four letters or less......would appear in the Code in the course of the permutation of the letters of the alphabet'. Later, when vowels were introduced, the flag intended for A was the same as the houseflag of T. & J. Brocklebank Ltd. (11) of Liverpool, one of the oldest of British shipping companies, with origins going back to about 1770. Brocklebanks were particularly proud of their houseflag and of their custom of flying it at the fore instead of the main, as was usual (the practice was by no means as unique as Brocklebank's pretended, as many a painting of nineteenth century sailing ships will show). They were approached to alter their flag, refused, and so the A flag is one of only two flags in the code which are swallowtailed. Incidentally, the houseflag in contention was not Brocklebank's original one, having been adopted in 1820, when it replaced a blue flag with a white ball (12). This earlier flag was still in use up to 1827, and paintings of the sailing vessels *Castor* and *Princess Charlotte* show them flying it - incidentally, at the main!

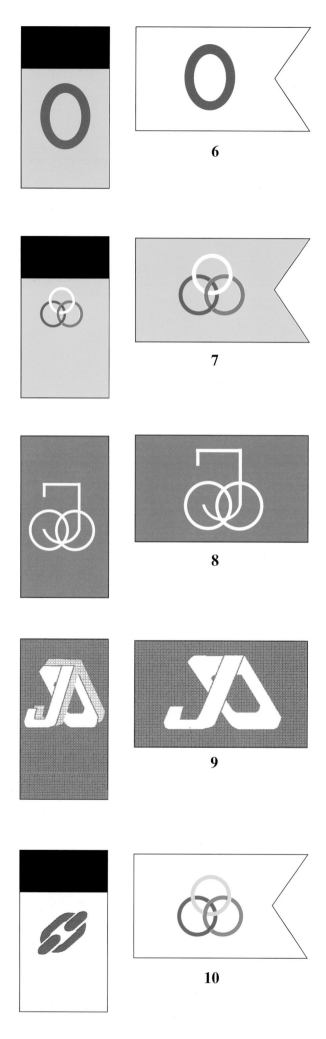

Odfjell's almost new *Bow Gran* (6,673/1970) displays funnel 7 very clearly in this 1971 photograph. In 1980, the chemical tanker was transferred to J.O. Odfjell A/S and was renamed *Jo Gran*. In 1983 she became the Liberian *Betula* but remained Norwegian-owned and management continued with J.O. Odfjell A/S until 1988. On 25th June 1993, began a chapter of accidents that those who crew and run chemical tankers must dread. During discharge at Lazaro Cardenas her highly corrosive cargo of sulphuric acid leaked into the pump room, so frightening the crew that they, perhaps prematurely, left the ship. Despite leaks and a list, she was towed out of port, but the abandoned ship was soon driven aground by a storm and in early July was rolled on to her side by a hurricane, causing even more of her cargo to spill. Given the potential environmental damage, no doubt the owners, Betula ANS, were glad that they had opted for single-ship company status. *[World Ship Photo*

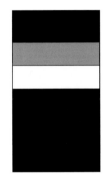

11

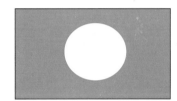

12

In May 1965, *Mangla* (8,805/1959) flies T. and J. Brocklebank's houseflag from her fore mast. The Port Glasgow-built *Mangla* was one of the classic British post-war cargo liner designs, but was doomed to a short life. She was sold to Marchessini Lines in 1972 to become *Eurypylus*, but an engine room explosion during November 1975 brought a premature end to her life, and she was broken up at Kaohsiung in 1976. *[George Gould collection, World Ship Photo Library 9909]*

Bibby's third *Derbyshire* (7,412/1965) enters the Nieuw Waterweg, at about 6.00 am on 22nd June 1976. Despite her conventional, midships superstructure, she and her sister were designed as bulk carriers. They had an unusually low freeboard, and because of this there was no access to the superstructure from the main deck. As if to emphasise their role, these two Doxford-built motorships were transferred from Bibby Line Ltd. to Bibby Bulk Carriers Ltd. in 1973.

This was almost certainly *Derbyshire's* last voyage for Bibby, as soon afterwards she was bought by the Greeks, who had such an appetite for ex-British cargo ships, becoming first *Captain Lygnos* and later *Chrysovalandrou*. On 24th November 1982 whilst on ballast passage from Piraeus to Poland, fire began in her engine room. Taken in tow, the fire was put out, but mysteriously started again, and was not extinguished until 6th December. The remains were later towed into Cartagena and broken up. *[Paul Boot]*

The only other swallowtailed flag in the International Code is the 'B' flag, which is plain red. It may not be entirely coincidental that the original houseflag of the Bibby Line Ltd. (13) of Liverpool was also a plain red one, and that this company, since Brocklebank's sold their last ships in 1983, is the longest-lived of British shipowners. John Bibby was in shipbroking from 1801 and set up in shipowning in 1807. From 1873 the company came under the control of the Leyland Line, but the family bought it back in 1889, and the plain red flag continued in use until 1926. At that time, the association of the red flag with the Bolshevik revolution in Russia had several times caused a stir in Continental ports when Bibby Line ships were seen flying it, so in 1926 the Bibby crest was added. The funnel is always stated to be a unique pinkish shade of buff, though in my memory of Bibby cargo liners in the 1960s, it was not very different from such as the Shaw Savill boats. Most certainly the gas and chemical tankers now operated by the company have a much paler, mundane shade. Nowhere have I found any reference to Bibby's refusing to alter their flag so that it could be used for the International Code, but we may be permitted to wonder.

The opposite situation, of shipowners using signal flags as the basis for their houseflags, has often happened. One of the best-remembered examples is probably Coast Lines Ltd. (14) the Liverpool-based amalgamation of the Bacon, Powell and Hough lines which, in the years between the wars and just after the Second World War absorbed almost every other company in the coastal liner trades, and many another coastal firm at that. After two earlier sets of markings, the company adopted in 1937 the 'C' flag of the International Code, defaced by its initials. Many Coast Lines subsidiaries retained separate markings, but for only one, so far as I know, was a similar style of flag and funnel adopted: chevron funnel mark and houseflag based on a signal flag. This was Link Line Ltd. (15) of Liverpool, which traded across the Irish Sea from Lancashire ports with containers in the early stages of containerisation during the 1960s and 1970s. Here the flag was the 'L' flag, with the company initials in the yellow chequer, while the chevron combined the red of England and the green of Ireland.

13

14

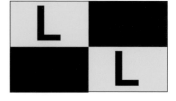

15

46

Spaniel (1,263/1955) is seen in the River Ribble in Link Line colours on 5th September 1964. Together with her sister *Pointer*, she was originally a bulk-carrying coaster, the two being built as *Brentfield* and *Birchfield* respectively. Early in their lives, however, owners Zillah Shipping and Carrying Co. Ltd. discovered they had made an expensive mistake in ordering these two ships, much bigger than the rest of their fleet. Owners Coast Lines Ltd. helped them out by taking them over in 1958 and converting them into unit-load carriers for their pioneering Irish Sea service. Although the title Link Line was used, the ships remained under the ownership of various Coast Lines, and later P & O, subsidiaries. In 1973, *Spaniel* was sold to become *Conister* of the Isle of Man Steam Packet Co. Ltd., continuing to work on the Irish Sea until broken up in Spain during 1981. *[World Ship Photo Library]*

The Cardigan Shipping Co. Ltd. (16) of London was a company originally managed by John Cory and Sons Ltd., of Cardiff, but after Cory ceased business about 1969 it came under the control of Odd Godager of Oslo. The flag and funnel were changed to the same pattern as Godager's, but as a concession, the C was placed on the ball instead of Godager's G. Or was it? During the 1970s and 1980s varying reports came in of the letter as a C and also as a G, and for some time I put them down to mistakes. However, the inconsistency was cleared up by a letter from a chief engineer with Godager, who informed me that the vessels were crewed sometimes by British, sometimes by Norwegian officers. When the bridge staff were Norwegian, a G was painted on the funnel; when they were British, a C. He himself solved the problem by having a G

16

on one side of the funnel and a C on the other. I offer this tale with all necessary scepticism, but have never heard of anything similar.

The British-flag *Norse Viking* (14,833/1970) was built in Sweden for a Norwegian owner, but registered in the United Kingdom and managed by Ropners. Fitted with removable car decks, she initially carried cargoes of up to 1,700 cars from Europe to North America, returning with grain, ore or scrap. In 1980 she was transferred by Odd Godager to a Liberian company and put under the Bahamas flag as *Norse Captain*. Sold out to Greek owners in 1983 as *Lydi*, she yet retained a tenuous British connection, as her registered owner was Bolton Trading Inc. *Lydi* arrived at Alang to be broken up in October 1997. *[George Gould collection, World Ship Photo Library]*

MORE BRITISH C1-M-AV1s

JUTAHY (above) and **SARGENT** (below)
Walter Butler Shipbuilders, Duluth, Minnesota, USA;
1945, 3,805gt, 339 feet overall
Oil engine 8-cyl. 2SCSA by Busch Sulzer Brothers Diesel
Engine Co., St Louis, Missouri, USA.

Correspondents Alan McLelland and David Asprey have pointed out that the articles on British C1-M-AV1s in *Record* 13 omitted two vessels owned by the Vestey Group. Neither were members of the group of ten chartered to the British Ministry of War Transport and given *Hickory*-names, and instead were bought by what were British-controlled, flag-of-convenience operators, later coming under British ownership.

Launched as *Frank J. Petrarca*, but completed with the knot name *Roband Hitch*, *Jutahy* was given this name when bought in 1946 by the Panama Shipping Co. Inc., of Panama. Along with *Pachitea*, she was chartered to the Booth Steamship Co. Ltd., and this immediately raises

suspicions that her owners were a subsidiary of the Vestey Group, who had acquired Booth early in 1946. However, only in later years does *Lloyd's Confidential Index* acknowledge links between Panama Shipping, Booth and Lamport & Holt. The names of both chartered ships came from tributaries of the Amazon; the former name is now spelt Jutaí.

Suspicions of a Vestey connection are confirmed by the acquisition of the ship by Lamport & Holt Line Ltd. in 1954, when she was renamed *Sargent* and registered in Port of Spain, Trinidad. Despite this oddball port, she seems to have engaged in most of Lamport & Holt's trades, including voyages to the United Kingdom. Sale in 1962 followed lay-up (probably since May 1959, when surveys fell due) and as *Pamit* and later *Bambero* she was owned in Greece. Early in March 1970 she arrived at Castellon, Spain to be broken up. *[Both: World Ship Photo Library, Brownell collection]*

DUNSTAN (above) and **SALLUST** (below)
Leathem D. Smith Shipbuilding Co., Sturgeon Bay,
Wisconsin, USA; 1945, 3,844gt, 339 feet overall
Oil engine 6-cyl. 4SCSA by the Nordberg Manufacturing
Co., Milwaukee, USA.
The name *Coastal Challenger*, under which this ship was
completed in May 1945, suggests that the United States
Maritime Commission may have given up the search for
the names of further obscure knots. She had been intended
to carry the name *Tulare* as a cargo ship for the US Navy.

She followed the same route into British
ownership as *Jutahy*, being bought by the Panama

Shipping Co. Inc. in 1947 and as *Pachitea* chartered to
Booths. However, the Liverpool company bought her in
1954 and renamed her *Dunstan*, registering her in their
home port. In 1959 she was transferred within the Vestey
Group to Lamport & Holt as *Sallust*, a year later moving on
to Austasia Line Ltd. as *Malacca*. Already trading in the
Far East, she was sold in 1962 to Kie Hock Shipping Co.
Ltd. of Hong Kong who named her *Tong Hong*. On 25th
October 1967, she left Kawasaki with ammonium sulphate
for Colombo and, in those fateful words, 'was never seen
again'. *[Above: Fotoflite incorporating Skyfotos]*

THEMES AND VARIATIONS:

THE DEVELOPMENT OF POST-WAR BANK LINE CARGO SHIPS PART 1
Paul Boot

Whilst 'Lloyd's Register of Shipping' currently lists over 30,000 ships, regrettably few of these could seriously be considered to have any aesthetic merit. Little more than thirty years ago the enthusiasm for conveying cargoes in boxes, or in ever larger bulk carriers, gathered an unstoppable momentum. A new generation of shipping was brought into being and with it came a new generation of owners to whom their ships were little more than anonymous assets on a balance sheet. As the commercial pressures for ever lower construction and operating costs increased, form became ever more subjugated to base functionality.

It is, on reflection, perhaps more remarkable that the traditional shipbuilding practices that gave vessels such pleasing, well-proportioned profiles, lasted for so long. Hulls with a gentle sheer line, cambered decks, a finely flared bow and a shaped, rounded, stern added considerably to the overall cost of construction. Many owners, more often associated with frugality than frippery, lavished yet further money on what were little more than stylish embellishments. A hardwood-fronted bridge and wheelhouse; a tapered, dome-topped funnel and even a white line cut in along the hull may all have looked very nice but they each came at a price and gave not a penny return on the expenditure. Indeed, some of the larger concerns sought also to impart a mark of individuality in design throughout their fleets, with the post-war constructions of the Blue Funnel and Glen Lines being inspired examples of the hand of their own naval architect. If other companies were perhaps less committed to this purpose, then the pedigree of their vessels was often still evident long after subsequent owners had substituted their own colours; even when this was sometimes predominately the rust staining of total neglect. Through long associations with a particular shipbuilder, a number of companies achieved some measure of distinction probably more by chance than design. Of these, Andrew Weir's Bank Line provides a particularly interesting example, not least for it having shared the orders for the greater part of its post-war reconstruction programme between just two builders. Weir was also amongst but a handful of owners to fully embrace the benefits of series production. From the design of an initial order of three conventional motorships delivered by William Doxford and Sons Ltd. in 1947 and 1948, a further 55 vessels were to evolve over the next twenty years. Of these, 27 were built by Doxford at their Sunderland yard and the remainder by Harland and Wolff Ltd. at Belfast.

With their pre-eminence in the development and construction of oil engines, these two builders had already established themselves with Bank Line during the inter-war years. In 1922 Andrew Weir, by then ennobled as Baron Inverforth of Southgate, had placed an order with Harland and Wolff for 21 motorships. This was then the largest single order constructed for any shipowner in peacetime. Not only was the size of this order exceptional, but so too was the timescale of less than thirty months within which the order was completed. It was a tremendous achievement for Harland's Govan yard and no less a remarkable demonstration of faith by Lord Inverforth in both the builders and this new technology. The average of over 33 years' service - war and other losses excluded - which each of these ships gave to the company, clearly demonstrated that his faith had been well founded.

If Doxford's contribution at this time was on a less heroic scale, it was not without significance. In the early years of the last century, these builders had been in the forefront of diesel engine development. During the depths of the depression of the 1930s, they had introduced the 'Economy Ship' whose principal selling feature was its three-cylinder opposed piston diesel engine. Producing 1,800 brake horsepower, this unit enabled a service speed of 11 knots to be achieved on a consumption of only 6$\frac{1}{2}$ tons of diesel oil a day. Designed principally to appeal to tramp ship owners, this standard ship design could be seen as a precursor of the SD14 type, conceived and built on the same river some thirty years later. Of the four Economy type ships that were ordered by Bank before the war, *Willowbank* of 1939 was the only one that had the basic three-cylinder engine. For the others, a more powerful four-cylinder engine was specified, raising the service speed to 12 knots.

At the outbreak of the Second World War motorships predominated, constituting exactly three quarters of Bank Line's 48 vessels. Only seven new ships were built for the company during the war, but all bar one of these were motorships, including four examples of the Doxford Economy 'Improved Series'. Welcome though these would have been, they did little to make good the loss of 25 vessels within those six years and it would be a long time before the fleet was rebuilt to something of its former strength and grandeur.

Peace, prosperity and pragmatism

The return to peace offered rich rewards to shipping companies but, with shipyards struggling to satisfy the demand, the extended delivery times and escalating prices deterred many from ordering new tonnage. Tramp ship operators especially, always the most vulnerable to depressed trading conditions, were still mindful of the long lean years that had soon followed in the wake of the First World War and most were reluctant to make this long term commitment. Bank Line, of course, had divided interests and, apart from its significant involvement in tramping, had its extensive liner services to consider. The very measured pace of the reconstruction programme would seem, therefore, to have been surprisingly cautious.

Doxfords were favoured with the company's initial peacetime order which was for just two sister ships, later increased to three. *Eastbank*, the first to enter service, was handed over at the end of 1947. Progression round the compass continued with the *Southbank*, handed over in March the following year, and the *Westbank* some eight months later Like the majority of the earlier Doxford motorships, they had a rather minimal, composite

Eastbank was the first new ship to be built for the company after the war, but even so she did not enter service until the end of 1947. In 1965 she was sold to one of the many concerns managed by Ramon de la Sota Junior, who renamed her *Bordazuri* under the Liberian flag. Subsequent sales brought further name changes, all carried under the Greek flag: *Pella* in 1972; *Sierra* in 1974; *Makedonia II* in 1977, as which she passed to Italian breakers who demolished her at La Spezia during 1980.

superstructure with an upright funnel; but the raised forecastle and poop gave them a more pleasing and well balanced profile which, in certain aspects of its styling, had a particular affinity with the Harland and Wolff-built *Shirrabank* of 1940. The five-cylinder, opposed-piston, diesel engine which developed 5,150 brake horse power, represented a considerable advance on the earlier Doxford machinery and allowed a service speed of 14 knots to be easily achieved.

They were conventional vessels, unpretentious even, in many ways no more than typical shelter-deck cargo ships of that era. Some measure of their ordinariness can be gleaned from the very meagre coverage they were accorded in the contemporary editions of that august journal, 'The Motor Ship', warranting just a column inch or two amongst the lavish reports on more exotic constructions of the time. One feature of particular note however, that was not immediately apparent, was the substantial deep tank capacity of over 2,800 tons for vegetable oils, in addition to which 138 tons of latex could be accommodated in the fore-peak tanks. Provision for liquid cargoes was an important facet of Bank's liner trades, which included products such as soya bean oil, mineral oils and additives from the United States Gulf ports to Australia; with coconut oil, and in later years palm oil, from the Pacific Islands to Europe. These were

difficult cargoes, requiring a high degree of cleanliness for the food grade oils and the joys of the regular manual cleaning out of the tanks between cargoes is best left to the imagination. Coated tanks and automated cleaning systems were then a long way away. The carriage of palm oil was especially demanding, as all brass valves and fittings had to be replaced with stainless steel parts. If these requirements were not enough, then maintaining the integrity of the tanks to prevent seepage was a perennial problem; in particular where, as with this class, the tank tops were riveted. Many an engineer must have cursed at having to work in these confined spaces.

Four years elapsed after the delivery of the *Westbank* before a further order for new tonnage was placed. In the interim second hand purchases, mainly Uncle Sam's Liberties augmented by a smaller number of Empire designs, largely made good the wartime losses. Whatever their shortcomings, the Liberty ships were inexpensive and they were readily available. Certainly, they proved to be good enough for the likes of Ellerman, Harrison, and Blue Funnel even, who all retained significant numbers of these mass produced basic steamships well into the 'fifties. Bank purchased a total of twelve Liberties, the largest number acquired by any British concern; eight of which they had previously managed on behalf of the Ministry of Transport whilst on

Although she was a product of the Harland and Wolff yard at Belfast, the 1940 built motorship *Shirrabank* had many similarities with the Doxford designs. The superstructure, in particular, would seem to have inspired the detailing of the later Sunderland-built *'Compass' banks*.

Unusually, *Shirrabank* was not sold for further trading and was delivered to Hong Kong breakers in September 1963. [Fotoflite, incorporating Skyfotos]

Beaverbank, was the lead ship of a class of three ordered from Harland and Wolff; their first order from Bank Line since the *Shirrabank* of 1940. In addition to the two sisterships, *Nessbank* and *Fleetbank*, also delivered in 1953, a further three, very similar, but marginally longer ships were completed two years later.

Beaverbank was sold in 1970 and thereafter flew the Greek flag for most of the remainder of her days, first as the *Eratini* and then, from 1972, *Provimi Star*. A transfer to the Panamanian register in 1981 preceded her sale to Pakistani breakers the following year.

bareboat charter from the United States. Steam power had returned with a vengeance, and it was not until 1958 that the motorship was to regain the level of its pre-war supremacy within the fleet.

Back to Belfast
Contrary to the more pessimistic predictions, the demand for dry cargo ships did not collapse as the post-war era advanced and, sustained to a degree by the Korean War in 1950, it was not until 1952 that trade suffered a significant, albeit brief, downturn. As the cost of newbuilding stabilised for a while - it had risen by 25% during 1951 alone - the company seized the opportunity to take another small step in its reconstruction programme. This time they returned to Harland and Wolff, placing an order with their Belfast yard for just three ships which were delivered in 1953. The *Beaverbank*, *Nessbank* and *Fleetbank* were dimensionally and ostensibly very similar to the Doxford trio completed five years earlier. Notable external detail differences were the larger diameter funnel with a raked top, and plain metal, rather than hardwood, facing to the bridge wings. One minor feature, which henceforth was to distinguish the products of these two builders, was the positioning of the name at the bow. On the Doxford built vessels, black lettering on the white 'half round' of the forecastle was uniformly applied, whilst Harlands standardised on white lettering on the black hull immediately below.

In terms of performance the two series were very similar, with the six-cylinder, Harland - Burmeister & Wain opposed piston engine producing a comparable output to the five-cylinder Doxford of the earlier ships. Three further ships, *Cedarbank*, *Foylebank* and *Laganbank*, almost identical but five feet longer overall, followed in 1955; the

year in which the company celebrated its seventieth anniversary and its founder, Andrew Weir, died. This was also the year in which the reconstruction programme finally got seriously underway. It was certainly not before time.

Although numerically the fleet had by then been all but restored to its former strength, only nine of the ships were less than ten years old. The average age of the remainder was over eighteen years; 16 of them were steamships, all but one of which were second-hand, war-time built acquisitions and, of the motorships, 13 were more than twenty five years old. Foremost amongst these was *Gujarat*, the lead ship of the original Harland order. When eventually sold in 1957, this 34-year old veteran had logged up nearly two million miles on her original engine and went on to give her new owners in Hong Kong a further four years' service.

Orders were placed for no fewer than 16 ships, divided equally between, Harland and Wolff Ltd. and Wm. Doxford and Sons. In both instances, these orders were subsequently increased to ten ships before the first had been completed. Of very similar dimensions and basic technical specifications, the two series were of very differing appearance. Harland's design was unmistakably a development of that of the *Beaverbank* and her sisters. The hull form was now enhanced by a fully formed cruiser stern, thus incorporating a feature that had become a hallmark of the majority of motorships built at this Belfast yard. Other minor differences were the raked funnel and an enclosed front to the superstructure; both imparting a more modern and harmonious conformation. The principal advancement though, was to be found in the engine room where the main machinery was a Harland - B & W, turbocharged six-cylinder engine, capable of running on heavy oil or diesel; the first installation of one of these engines in a general cargo vessel. On trials, *Cloverbank*,

the first of what would ultimately be a total of twelve identical sisterships, put up an impressive performance, achieving a tad under 19 knots on one run over the measured mile. In service, however, $14^1/_2$ knots was deemed to be quite sufficient. *Cloverbank* also brought to an end the long standing tradition of registering the Belfast built ships in that city. Like the remainder of the fleet she, and all her Harland built successors, now took Glasgow as their port of registration.

Whereas Harlands had stuck closely to the script, Doxford launched out in a somewhat different direction in their design. Forsaking, in the main, a raised poop - the crew's accommodation aft was now situated in the 'tween deck space - the hull lines were taken smoothly up into the forecastle through elegant extended hances, complemented by a curved, well raked stem. This flowing styling was echoed in the superstructure, with a subtly rounded, raked profile at the fore complementing the long sweeping arc of the plating below the bridge wings carried down to the boat deck. As the ocean liner had reached the pinnacle of its design in the inter-war years, so the cargo ship rose to its zenith in the 'fifties and 'sixties. Lest it be thought that an appreciation of the shipping of that era has come about only with the passing of time, a contemporary report waxed lyrical on the effect of good modern design. Writing in a special supplement published by the 'The Journal of Commerce' newspaper to mark the company's seventieth anniversary, Dr. J. Ramsay Gebbie, the managing director of Doxfords, noted that '... it makes me happy to know that the shipowner of to-day, although primarily concerned with the earning power of a ship, still likes to own a beautiful and graceful vessel. Truly I believe that the romance of the old sailing ship days has returned with such ships'. His company had, of course, just received this large and valuable order from Bank Line.

Osia Irini Chrysovalandou II (opposite), formerly the *Fleetbank*, built in 1953, would be well placed amongst the contenders for the longest ship's name. Whilst she looks to be exceptionally well kept, seen here sailing fully laden from Rotterdam, she was to end her career in ignominy.

Having loaded a cargo of sugar at Rotterdam for Tunisia early in 1978, she next appeared under an assumed new

identity as the *Camelia* at the Lebanese port of Sidon where she was seized by the authorities. Sent back to Tunisia to discharge her cargo at La Goulette she then proceeded to Bizerta where she languished for the next five years, finally being broken up there in 1983.
[J. Krayenbosch/Paul Boot]

Avonbank (above) was the penultimate ship to be completed of this group of a dozen identical sisters and still projects a powerful image nearly a decade and a half later as she makes an early morning arrival at Rotterdam in May 1975. She was sold two years later to Panamanian buyers becoming *Fortune Star* as which she was broken up in China in 1984. *[Malcolm Cranfield/Paul Boot]*

The styling of the Doxford series built from 1957 onwards was a radical departure from this yard's earlier designs. *Riverbank* entered service just three months after the prototype, *Firbank*. She was sold to Guan Guan Shipping (Pte) Ltd., in 1974 and, as the *Golden Season*, she sailed in their distinctive colours until 1985, when she was delivered to Chinese breakers at Huangpu. This superb aerial view of *Riverbank* in her prime shows much of the deck and superstructure arrangement of the first of what would be many variants within this group of 21 vessels.

[Fotoflite incorporating Skyfotos]

There were some significant differences among the first five members of this Doxford-built group. With her raised poop, additional hatchway and derricks, as well as a six-cylinder engine, *Northbank* was unique. In other respects though, her styling closely followed that of her contemporaries.

Sold in 1973, after a typical sixteen years' service she passed into the hands of the Papalios group of companies where she briefly joined many other vessels acquired from the rapidly diminishing British merchant fleet. She was to carry her new name *Aegis Lion* for only a few months as, in August of that year, she stranded near Punta Arenas and sank a couple of days later.

Of no less significance was the method of construction. Doxfords had not only been pioneers in oil engine development, but had also been early exponents of electric arc welding. Their hulls, therefore, were extensively welded, as of course was much else, in contrast to the Harland-built series in which riveting predominated. Might these different construction techniques have influenced the variance in the styling; the former allowing an expressive flair, the latter fostering a more formal and classic line?

The difference is in the detail

Unlike their Belfast built cousins, the Sunderland family underwent a continuing evolution in their styling and equipment as the series progressed. To attempt to record in detail each and every one of the many variations would risk entering into the realms of what is sometimes referred to as 'rivet counting'. The following observations outlining some of the principal differences are thus intended to provide a linking commentary on the accompanying photographs and profile drawings.

Firbank was the first of the Doxford order to be completed, in January 1957, followed by *Riverbank*, three months later. *Northbank*, the third in this series, handed over in June that year was something of a oddity, having not only a raised poop construction embracing the aftermost hatchway with an additional pair of kingposts and derricks, but a six-cylinder Doxford engine in place of the four-cylinder model otherwise installed throughout this group. It would seem that this larger engine had become available from a cancelled order and was offered by the builders in the hope that similar units might be specified for future orders. Despite the significantly increased power this engine provided, *Northbank's* service speed was limited to 15 knots; just half a knot greater than her consorts. *Birchbank* and *Streambank*, which were delivered the year after, both had mechanically operated hatch covers on the weather deck. The raised winch houses and platforms, necessary to accommodate the covers in their stowed position, were a more obvious manifestation of this particular variation. This feature did not find favour

Streambank, and her immediate predecessor *Birchbank*, were the only two ships within this group to be equipped with mechanically operated hatch covers. The raised, extended winch platforms made for easy recognition of this pair, which otherwise differed little from their peers.

Streambank had the rare distinction, however, of being sold on to other British owners, R I Management and R I Shipping Ltd. and joined the Runciman fleet as *Fernmoor* in 1971. Sold again in 1973, she became *Banglar Polyxeni*, carrying the livery of the Bangladesh Shipping

Corporation, but under Greek ownership. In 1977 the name was foreshortened to *Polyxeni*. Yet a further sale, in 1982, saw her trading for a short while as the Maltese flagged *Intra Triumph*, as which she was broken up at Gadani Beach the following year. *[Fotoflite incorporating Skyfotos]*

Lindenbank (top), built in 1961, came exactly midway through this extensive group and thus represents an intermediate form of the evolution of the design. The slightly foreshortened superstructure now has a composite funnel housing, with the lifeboats raised on luffing davits. Fore and main topmasts are still carried and, at the stern, the bulwarks are still fully plated. She has yet to receive the lattice tie beam modification to the head of the forward kingposts.

Lindenbank was to meet an untimely end in August 1975 when she was wrecked off Fanning Island in the Western Pacific during a voyage from Kimbe to the United Kingdom.   [Malcolm Cranfield]

With her raised poop, incorporating an additional hatchway served by an extra pair of derricks, *Trentbank* (middle) was one of only three ships within the group to sport this feature. Her identical sister, *Forresbank*, was the third. Was there any other series design ever produced in which a raised poop came as something of an optional extra?

Trentbank also marks the next phase in the evolution of the superstructure styling. The bridge island has now been extended and integrated into the wheelhouse with the plating faired over from the top of the bridge. On this, a larger signal mast carrying the radar scanner and navigational lights has replaced the fore and main topmasts.

Trentbank was to have a miserably short career. Little more than two years after completion, she was in collision with the Portugese tanker *Fogo* (17,758/1958) about 70 miles north west of Alexandria whilst on passage from Australia to Liverpool. The Liberian tanker *Harold A. Helm* (51,320/1958) took her in tow the following day, and she arrived off Port Said on the 23rd September 1964. The next day she foundered offshore and was declared a constructive loss. Salvors succeeded to refloat the hulk two years later. The hull was towed, keel up, to Ambelaki and was demolished at Piraeus

Laurelbank (bottom) incorporates further detail variations, most noticeably in this view, the open railings around the stern. These would have provided a far greater freeing area for water shipped in a heavy following sea. Other detail differences are the single stump mast forward, in place of the twin kingposts, and the rounded back to the funnel.

Sold in 1979, *Laurelbank* became the *Vali Pero* and after a five-year lay up at Calcutta, she was scrapped there in 1990.
[Paul Boot]

at that time, however, and *Teakbank*, the next to enter service, reverted to traditional boarded hatch covers, and minimal mast houses, as did all subsequent vessels in this group. The *Wavebank* and *Yewbank* were followed by the two additional vessels to the original order, *Willowbank* and *Larchbank*, completed in 1960 and 1961 respectively, which introduced a minor change in the layout of the superstructure. In the earlier vessels, the funnel had been positioned on a separate casing on the boat deck, separated from the bridge structure by the engine room skylights. A concession, perhaps, to the end of the era of the once ubiquitous, split-superstructure configuration? This casing was now extended and incorporated into the main structure, enabling the lifeboats to be raised above the deck on luffing davits.

By now yet further orders had been placed and ultimately no fewer than 21 vessels were built to this basic design. *Lindenbank*, *Weirbank* and *Testbank* followed at almost monthly intervals towards the end of 1961, the latter incorporating several more modifications. Fore and main top masts were dispensed with, and in their place a larger, styled, combined signal and radar mast was provided on the bridge island which was now enhanced by faired plating; the superstructure was slightly foreshortened; the funnel re-styled; and around the stern, open railings were substituted for the fully-plated bulwarks. More importantly perhaps, *Testbank* was the first to be powered by the Doxford 'P' type turbo-charged engine, with an output of 6,640 brake horsepower.

Deliveries continued apace through the first part of 1962. *Inverbank* commissioned in March was a repeat of her predecessor. *Forresbank* and *Trentbank,* completed soon after, adopted the same styling, yet strangely saw the return of the raised poop and its appurtenances. This feature would, at least, have afforded some small improvement to the crew's accommodation, which was now raised above the level of the weather deck. Within this cramped enclave lived a peripatetic, ethnic community whose designations now give little clue to their role in the day-to-day life of these ships. Bhandaries, Donkeymen, Seacunnies, Serangs, Topazes, Tindals and Cassabs; 35 souls in all; more than the

complement of most modern freighters many times the size of these modest cargo ships. More practically, however, the poop would have enhanced the seaworthiness of these vessels in a following sea. The change to open railings round the stern, as noted earlier, suggests that the aft deck may have got uncomfortably wet in these conditions. It certainly allowed these sisters to be loaded to a deeper draught, even if this was little more than one whole inch.

After a respite of some eight months, the Sunderland yard got into its stride again completing *Oakbank* in March, *Rowanbank* in May and *Laurelbank* in August of 1963. A minor distinguishing detail of this trio was the rounded, rather than squared off back to the top of the funnel. Like the 'pooped' sisters that had preceded them, the heavy-lift derricks mounted on their foremasts had a capacity of 50 tons; 20 tons greater than earlier examples. *Laurelbank* introduced a further minor modification in the form of a single mast, with a crosstree, between the second and third hatchways, in place of the twin, plain posts that had hitherto been the norm. These had reportedly suffered from vibration - most likely a harmonic resonance in the manner of a gigantic tuning fork - and to counteract this, a lattice tie beam had been installed between the head of the posts on the earlier vessels. Although a larger development of this class appeared later in 1963, two further and final variants of the original design were added to the fleet the following year.

There is, arguably, no single element that defines the character of a ship so much as the funnel and the heavily styled and rakish version, incorporating the signal mast, gave both *Hollybank* and *Sprucebank* a markedly different disposition to their predecessors. The positioning of the funnel further forward, and combined into the bridge structure, reinforced this effect, as did the much narrower, inclined black top applied. Of the host of detail variations applied over the seven years spanning the construction of this group, this was among the more minor, yet certainly was the most striking.

To be concluded in *Record* 18 with drawings and details of the Harland and Wolff-built ships.

With her styled funnel, *Hollybank*, together with her sister *Sprucebank*, stood out from the rest of this large, Doxford-built group. Although the pair may initially appear to belong to a completely different class, a closer inspection reveals that all the principal elements of the original design are still present. They represented the culmination of the seven year evolution of

this group and the styling of the superstructure was adopted for two series of larger developments of the design which were built between 1964 and 1967.

Hollybank's sale in 1979 reflected the growing dominance of containerisation. Greek buyers put her under the Panamanian flag as the *Nikitas F.* as which she traded for only two years.

Sold without change of name in 1981, she was to spend the next eight years laid up at Piraeus, during which time she was sold on again in 1987, hoisting the Maltese flag as *Nonos*. She was to make just one more voyage, at the end of 1989, which ultimately took her to the breakers' yards at Alang early in 1990.

Vessels built by Wm. Doxford and Sons Ltd. *and*
Doxford and Sunderland Shipbuilding and Engineering Co. Ltd.
Between 1947 - 1967

Type D1

Length (o.a.): 464'   Breadth: 60' 0"   Main engine: Doxford 5-cyl, opposed piston

	Completed	Tonnage Gross	Tonnage Deadweight	Notes / Distinguishing features
EASTBANK	12.1947	5,947*	9,325*	
SOUTHBANK	3.1948	5,957*	9,325*	
WESTBANK	11.1948	5,957*	9,325*	

Type D2

Length (o.a.): 487/488'   Breadth: 62'3"   Main engine: Doxford, 4-cyl, opposed piston (E^4) - 'P' Type (E^4P)
Doxford, 6-cyl, opposed piston (E^6)

	Completed	Gross	Deadweight	Engine	Hull	S/struct	Masts	Deck
FIRBANK	1.1957	6,318*	10,450*	E^4	H1/a	S1	fm-tk	
RIVERBANK	4.1957	6,318*	10,450*	E^4	H1/a	S1	fm-tk	
NORTHBANK	6.1957	8,504	12,000	E^6	H2	S1	fm-tk	
BIRCHBANK	5.1958	8,523	12,000	E^4	H1/a	S1	fm-tk	mh/wh
STREAMBANK	11.1968	8,520	12,100	E^4	H1/a	S1	fm-tk	mh/wh
TEAKBANK	12.1958	8,474	12,100	E^4	H1/a	S1	fm-tk	
WAVEBANK	2.1959	8,473	12,100	E^4	H1/a	S1	fm-tk	
YEWBANK	4.1959	8,473	12,100	E^4	H1/a	S1	fm-tk	
WILLOWBANK	7.1960	6,335*	10,143*	E^4	H1/a	S2	fm-tk	
LARCHBANK	7.1961	8,543	10,200*	E^4	H1/a	S2	fm-tk	
LINDENBANK	9.1961	8,541	10,200*	E^4	H1/a	S2	fm-tk	
WEIRBANK	11.1961	6,354*	10,200*	E^4	H1/a	S2	fm-tk	
TESTBANK	12.1961	6,313*	10,355*	E^4P	H1/b	S3	sm-tk	
INVERBANK	3.1962	6,288*	10,355*	E^4P	H1/b	S3	sm-tk	
FORRESBANK	5 1962	6,310*	10,317*	E^4P	H2	S3	sm-tk	
TRENTBANK	7.1962	6,310*	10,317*	E^4P	H2	S3	sm-tk	
OAKBANK	3.1963	6,308*	10,405*	E^4P	H1/b	S3R	sm-tk	
ROWANBANK	5 1963	6,308*	10,405*	E^4P	H1/b	S3R	sm-tk	
LAURELBANK	8.1963	6,308*	10,405*	E^4P	H1/b	S3R	sm-sk	
HOLLYBANK	4.1964	8,566	12,190	E^4P	H1/b	S4	sm-sk	
SPRUCEBANK	8.1964	8,566	12,310	E^4P	H1/b	S4	sm-sk	

Type D3/1

Length (o.a.): 508'   Breadth: 67' 3"   Main engine: Doxford, 4-cyl. opposed piston   ('P' Type)

	Completed	Gross	Deadweight		
TAYBANK	12.1963	10,251	15,000		S4
TWEEDBANK	1.1964	10,251	15,000		S4
BEECHBANK	4.1965	10,221	15,000		S5
ERNEBANK	7.1965	10,222	15,000		S5

Type D3/2   (Built by: **Doxford and Sunderland Shipbuilding and Engineering Co. Ltd.**)

Length (o.a.): 528'   Breadth: 69' 4"   Main engine: Doxford, 6-cyl. opposed piston   ('J' Type)

	Completed	Gross	Deadweight		
SHIRRABANK	9.1966	10,439	15,150		S5
TEVIOTBANK	4.1967	10,439	15,150		S5

Key

*	Tonnage measured as completed as an open shelterdecker
H1/a	Hull with flush decked stern and plated bulwarks
H1/b	Hull with flush decked stern and open railings
H2	Hull with raised poop
S1	Funnel with upright back, on separe deckhouse
S2	Funnel with upright back, on composite supersstructure
S3	Tapered funnel (S3R - rounded top at back)
S4	'Styled' funnel incorporated into bridge house
S5	As S4, but with enclosed bridge deck

fm	Fore and main top-masts	- tk	Twin king posts for'rd
sm	Signal mast	-sk	Single king post for'rd
mh/wh	Mechanically operated hatch covers and large winch houses		

Notes

The type designations used here are not official and have been adopted solely for reference purposes in these tables and profile drawings.

The four 'D2 ' type vessels illustrated in the profile drawings on the opposite page have been chosen to illustrate all of the variations within this group. The configuration of individual vessels is as listed above in the 'Notes/distinguishing features' column.

The Doxford Vessels
Types D1 - D3

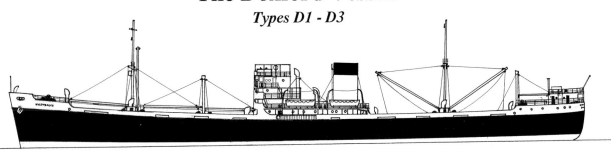

Type D1 EASTBANK (As built, with bulwarks painted white)

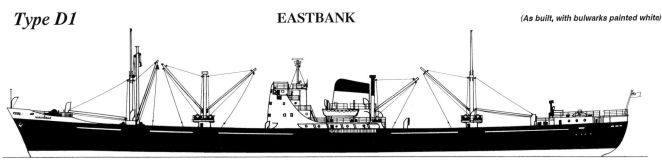

BIRCHBANK

Standard hull, with plated bulwarks at stern [H1/a]
Funnel with upright back, on separate deckhouse [S1]
Fore and main top masts [fm]
Raised and extended winch houses [mhw]

WEIRBANK

Standard hull, with plated bulwarks at stern [H1/a]
Funnel with upright back, on composite deckhouse [S2]
Fore and main top masts [fm]

D2 Types

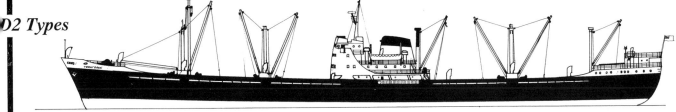

FORRESBANK

Hull with raised poop [H2]
Tapered funnel on composite deckhouse [S3]
Signal mast in place of fore and main top masts [sm]

HOLLYBANK

Standard hull, with open railings at stern [H1/b]
Styled funnel with signal mast incorporated into bridge house [S4]

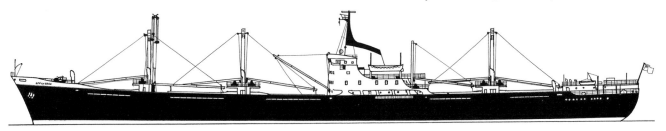

Type D3/1 BEECHBANK Superstructure with enclosed bridge deck [S5]
(Type D3/2 similar longer hull)

TWO FUNNEL POSTSCRIPT
- GLENOGLE OF 1882
Malcolm Cooper

Thomas Skinner's *Stirling Castle*, featured in *Record* 15, page 172, was only one of a pair of two-funnel cargo vessels introduced on to the UK to Far East service in 1882. Her rival, *Glenogle* of McGregor, Gow and Company's Glen Line, was not as fast and did not attract the same attention from the contemporary press. Although considered something of a failure, both at the time and by most subsequent historians, she actually fulfilled her designed role far more successfully than Skinner's flyer. While *Stirling Castle* proved so cripplingly expensive to run that Skinner was forced to sell her after only two years, *Glenogle* stayed on Glen Line's London to China service for over 20 years. After her eventual sale, she lasted another decade and a half in Far Eastern waters under a succession of local owners. She did not, however, retain her two-funnel configuration for very long, and as far as this author is aware, we are dependent on paintings to know what she looked like when she first left her builders.

Glenogle was launched by the London and Glasgow Engineering and Iron Shipbuilding Company of Glasgow in 1882. Coincidentally, London and Glasgow's Govan yard was almost alongside that of John Elder and Company, where Stirling Castle was built at almost exactly the same time. Glenogle was the twelfth vessel built by the company for the Glen Line. Indeed, apart from Glenorchy, which had been bought second hand in 1876, Gleniffer which was purchased on the stocks a year later, London and Glasgow had built all of Glen's steamer fleet. These ships had grown gradually in size and power from Glengyle of 1870 (1,667g 1,264n 274.2 x 32.9 x 24.4 feet. C2-cyl, cylinders 34/60 x 39 inches stroke; 185 NHP) to Glenavon of 1881 (2,985g 1,936g 360.4 x 43.3 x 24.5 feet. C2-cyl, cylinders 48/88 x 54 inches stroke; 530 NHP).

Glenogle (3,749g 2,000n 420.5 x 45.1 x 25.3 feet. C2-cyl, cylinders 59/83 x 60 inches stroke; 700 NHP) marked an attempt to accelerate this evolutionary design pattern. She was 60 feet longer and 25% larger by gross tonnage measure than Glenavon, and her engines had a 32% higher nominal horsepower rating. She was slightly longer than Stirling Castle, but five feet smaller on both breadth and depth. The biggest difference between the two vessels, however, was the engines. Stirling Castle's were far larger, and actually rated at a nominal horsepower of 1,500. It was this difference in engine power that was the cause of the significant difference in the two ships' careers.

On her first homeward China tea voyage in 1882, Stirling Castle made the passage from off Woosung to London in 30 days, a staggering seven days less than the previous year's record of 37 days set by Glen Line's Glencoe. In 1883, when extra drafts of stokers were carried in the search for even more speed, Stirling Castle took another day off the record. Glenogle, which had left Hankow 36 hours earlier, actually arrived four days later. Glenogle's 35 day passage was only a few days better than those managed by the older and smaller vessels in the fleet. As Glenogle was roughly 50% more expensive to build than her predecessors, she was not judged to have been a successful experiment. Glen did not build any further ships

like her. The next two additions to the fleet, Glengarry and Glenelg (both of which were delivered by London and Glasgow in 1883), reverted to the same basic hull size and engine capacity as Glenavon of 1881. Indeed, Glenogle was not matched for size in the Glen fleet until the mid-1890s, and not actually beaten for length until 1914.

It is clear, however, that Glenogle was not completely unprofitable on her designed service. Stirling Castle had to be sold quickly as her owner could not afford her huge operating losses. Glenogle carried on, although she lost her second funnel, probably when she was re-engined with more economical triple-expansion engines by her builder in 1890. A significant proportion of Glen Line's voyage results from the late nineteenth century survive, and it is possible to evaluate Glenogle's performance against that of some of the smaller vessels which entered the fleet around the same time.

Glenfruin and her sister Glenavon both entered service in 1881. Each had completed two voyages before Glenogle first sailed, but neither was to last as long in the fleet. Glenfruin was sold to McIlwraith and McEachern in 1897 for £16,500. Glenavon was wrecked at the end of 1898. The figures below cover all voyage results up to and including 1897. While they flatter the earlier pair slightly because of their head start in service, this is balanced by Glenogle's high earnings on one voyage in 1885-6, when she was actually chartered for naval service. Glenogle was converted into an armed merchant cruiser at Hong Kong in late 1885 and converted back for commercial use at the same port in 1886. The total paid to Glen Line for the naval hire was £25,305.15.0, and the company showed a profit on the 'voyage' of £21,857.4.7. Calculations for return on investment are not final ones as they do not include the proceeds of final sale/underwriters' payments, or the last

five and a half years of Glenogle's fleet life, but they do give a fair indication of the ships' performance up to 1897.

These figures show that Glenogle was not as profitable as the smaller pair of vessels that preceded her into service, and are sufficient to support management's own decision to revert to the older type with subsequent fleet additions. While she did not earn a very high return on investment, however, she did not actually lose her owners money. It was for this reason that she stayed on her designed service with her original owners, while her over-engined rival was quickly sold and spent most of her life as a South Atlantic passenger ship. In addition, the famous China tea races, which had spawned so many famous clipper ships and loomed so large in the early days of steam, lost their importance in the mid-1880s. China tea lost its place of prominence with the British consumer to its stronger tasting Indian rivals. As the Far Eastern shipping business moved on to other cargoes, the need for speed to attract premium freights gave way to the search for economy more widely associated with the development of the commercial steamship.

As has already been mentioned, Glenogle was converted to triple expansion in 1890. The refit cost her owners £15,000, but the ship then served on with them until 1903. In August of that year she was sold for £17,500 to Seang, Taik and Co. of Rangoon, acting on behalf of Lim Chin Tsong, also of Rangoon. In 1904, her Glasgow register was closed, and she was re-registered at Rangoon. Her new owner employed her on a variety of Far Eastern cargo services, ranging from India through south east Asia to China. She survived the First World War, but was finally wrecked on Syriam Flats in the river near her home port on 17th January 1919. She retained her original name throughout her entire 37 year life-span.

	Glenfruin	Glenavon	Glenogle
Built	1881	1881	1882
Cost	£56,114	£55,945	£90,123
Voyage profits to 1897	£77,831	£81,973	£108,695
New engines and surveys	£12,369	£14,368	£16,039
Net voyage profits	£65,462	£67,605	£92,656
Net surplus over cost	£9,348	£11,660	£2,533
Net return on investment	16.7%	20.8%	2.8%

PUTTING THE RECORD STRAIGHT

Letters, additions, amendments and photographs relating to articles in any issues of *Record* are welcomed. Letters may be lightly edited.

IRO irate

Your article 'Gone East' (*Record* 16) mentions a very interesting selection of ships. May I add a little further comment on two of these, both of which had been involved in the transportation of refugees after the Second World War?

Djakarta Raya had, as you say, been the *San Francisco* of the Republic Steamship Corporation of Panama in 1948. It was a time when the International Refugee Organisation (the IRO) were faced with the task of shipping over one million displaced persons from the continent of Europe to new lives elsewhere - often in North or South America or in Australasia. Many passenger ships had been lost during the Second World War and the shipyards were only slowly returning to full production, so there was a terrible shortage of vessels suitable for their purposes. The gap was partially filled by American troopships but, even so, the IRO had to shop around for whatever ships it could find. Opportunist shipowners were eager to cash in on the situation and scoured the world for vessels, however old or decrepit, which they could turn into emigrant ships and charter to the IRO.

Some owners who later became members of the shipping establishment got their start in the passenger trades in this way - including Achille Lauro, his nephews the Grimaldi brothers, the Costa family, Evgen Evgenides of Home Lines and Alexandre Vlasov of Sitmar. Not all the new entrants were so respectable, however. In April, 1949, a Federal Court Judge in Baltimore described the charter of the *San Francisco* to the IRO as 'one of the greatest fiascos ever to come into the court in the form of an Admiralty case'.

The IRO had, it seems, advanced $840,000 to Jose Madeiros, acting on behalf of the Republic Steamship Corporation, to convert the ship to a refugee-carrier. The corporation, it emerged, had not actually owned her at the time and had used $450,000 of the money to buy her. In the end, they were unable to complete the conversion and deliver her to the IRO as agreed. In the court case, the IRO sued for a total of $1,180,000 and the Maryland Drydock Co. sued for $860,970. Whether they ever got it is doubtful. The *San Francisco* passed into the ownership of the Maryland Drydock Co. and, after two years, was sold on to Djakarta Lloyd, as mentioned in the article.

Also mentioned, briefly, is the standard G-type cargo ship of 1918 which became the White Star *Gallic* and later the Clan Line's *Clan Colquhoun* (she had started life as the *War Argus*). She ended up as the Djakarta Lloyd's *Iman Bondjel* and later *Djatinegara*, but between 1947 and 1951 she had belonged to companies owned by the London Greeks John Livanos & Sons. At first they ran her as the freighter *Ioannis Livanos* but in 1949 she was converted for emigrant service and was renamed *Jenny*. Shortly before being sold to the Indonesians, she was chartered to the British Ministry of Transport for a few trooping voyages.
ANTHONY COOKE, Unit 212, Station House, 49, Greenwich High Road, London, SE10 8JL.

Drum Line revisited

The article on the *Omega* (*Record* 8, page 228) interested me as I have recently been researching Gillison and Chadwick's *Drumeltan*. Regarding the controversy of whether built as a ship or barque; if the original Inspection Certificate can be viewed I think the mast dimensions might resolve the issue. In the case of the *Drumeltan*, the fore, main and mizzen were of identical dimensions - lower masts of approximately 30 inch diameter. The jigger mast was 24 inch diameter, obviously not built to carry the same sail-load. 'Lloyd's Register' has her built as a ship, but pictures indicate a barque's jigger mast. Readers might be interested to know that the remains of the *Drumrock* are still visible in Takush Harbour, Smith Inlet. Just the mid-section of the hull - a lower mast and cross-trees - still stood twenty years ago. Wrecked as a barge about 1920, she gave her name to the rock on which she stranded.
JOHN M. ANDERSON, 1327 Chan Place, Victoria, British Columbia V9B 4J5, Canada

Beavan not Beaver

You'll probably have received a number of responses to the comment in Louis Loughran's letter on page 246 of *Record* 16 about the name of the Lord Mayor of Liverpool, where he gives it as 'Beaver'. The lady in question was Miss Margaret Beavan and she was a noted reformer of her day as well as being a pioneer female in local politics. I believe that she was related to the Beavan of Beavan Maples, commercial property specialists.

A minor point, but it gives me the opportunity to express my congratulations on the way that Ships in Focus *Record* has developed into a very fine canon of maritime history and research. I can best say that it equals 'Sea Breezes' at its most valuable (circa 1950 to 1975) before it took up its more populist approach to matters maritime.
JOHN GOBLE, john.goble@consignia.com

White-powered, under-powered

I was interested in the article on the White engine in *Record* 16. In the South American Saint Line we always thought that the White-engined ships were underpowered, only able to maintain 10 knots in favourable weather conditions. In the office, voyage estimates for these ships were always worked on the basis of a 9 knot service speed. After completing discharge in the UK, the ships had to make light passages to Antwerp for outward loading. Without deep tanks for ballast and with poor propeller immersion they were often in trouble in bad weather off the Dutch coast.

The inadequacy of the power unit was made all too plain to the crew of the *St. Clears* in 1947 when the new main engine was delivered to the ship on the back of a lorry.
D.L. STREET, 50 Hollybush Road, Cyncoed, Cardiff CF23 6TA

Recycled engines

Replying to David Burrell's question on page 180 of *Record* 15, 'From whence came these engines?' The *Toiler's* recycled engines came from steamers *D.C. Whitney* and *Simla*, the latter a 'stemwinder' (a salt-water sailor's term for a laker, which had a pilot house at the forward end).

D.C. Whitney was built in 1882 by Simon Langell Shipyard, St.Clair, Michigan for the Gilchrist Transportation Company. Built of oak, her dimensions were 240' x 40' x 23', 1,090g. She was deepened 6' 6" by the Detroit Dry Dock, Wyandotte, Michigan in 1885. Sold 1908 to Midland Towing and Wrecking Company (O.N. 122435) and renamed *Gargantua* (after a town in Canada) and reduced to a lighter. At this time her engines were probably removed. She was idle after 1914 and in 1920 was sold for non-transportation use as a floating dry dock.

Simla was built 1903 by the Calvin Company, Garden Island, Ontario, Canada for the Calvin Company (D.D. Calvin, manager). The dimensions of her composite hull were 230' 8" x 34'8" x 15", 1,490 gt. (O.N. 112114). She was named after the town state of Himachal, Pradesh, India. Ownership: 1903: Calvin Company, Kingston; 1915: Montreal Transportation Co., Ltd. Kingston, Montreal; 1921: Canada Steamship Lines Ltd., Montreal. Sold 1926 for one dollar to J. Donnelley, Montreal. Burned, stripped and scuttled on 8th November 1926 off Kingston, Ontario, Canada.
JOHN WILTERDING JUNIOR, 1529 Clark St., Algoma, Wisconsin 54201-1841, USA

Subjects in sixteen

Record 16 arrived at the end of last week and I have spent a thoroughly satisfying weekend devouring its contents. It was a great idea to concentrate in this issue on the often neglected field of marine engineering. A few matters for comment.
Page 207: An extra nought seems to have crept into the cost of the *Huntsman*. She actually cost £400,000. I suspect that £4,000,000 would have bankrupted Harrisons (and any other shipping company) in 1921.
Page 212. *Ventnor*: The text gives the wrong impression. Chelsea is the site of the only sugar refinery in New Zealand, some distance up the Waitemata harbour from the main Auckland city wharves. The *Ventnor* brought a cargo of raw sugar from Java, but the only coal handled at Chelsea was what was landed inward as fuel for the sugar mill boilers. The *Ventnor* loaded her coal at Westport and the bodies at Wellington. The text has a

strange spelling of Strait. Cook Strait, as any navigator will know, is anything but straight.

Page 225. The Battle of the Falkland Islands took place on 8th December 1914, not 'early in 1915'. SMS *Leipzig* was destroyed by HMS *Cornwall*, sinking at 9 pm on that day.

Page 234. *Liu Hai 2*: Kockums never had a Sulzer licence. The engines of the *Amazonas* were of MAN design - see *Ngomei Chou* on the next page.

Page 239. The Norwegian South American Line was not an Olsen subsidiary. It was a joint venture with Bergen Steam Ship Co. and Mowinckels (at the time in question).

Page 246. The flying of the City of Liverpool flag was not confined to when the Lamport and Holt ships were in Liverpool. The *Defoe* flew it from the stem when in Auckland in the early 1950s.

Page 248. The story of the *Stirling Castle* and her names is actually more complicated still. She DID carry both *Stirling Castle* and *Nord America* at the same time, though whether this was in the process of changing her name, I am not sure. There is photographic proof - in the 'Meccano Magazine' for October 1948 at page 342 which shows both names.

Page 258. There is only one 'N' in the first syllable of the *Kenkon Maru's* name.
BILL LAXON, Waimarana, Upper Whangateau Road, PO Box 171, Matakana 1240, New Zealand.

£400,000 was the correct price for Huntsman: thanks also to Ron Mapplebeck, Graeme Cubbin and Tony Smythe for pointing this out. Apparently, the name Stirling Castle was considered so famous that when under Italian ownership as Nord America she painted both names up. We hope to include more on Skinner's Castles in a forthcoming edition - see also Malcolm Cooper's article on page 60 and the request on page 64. Ed.

On page 200 of *Record 16* the final sentence is not very clear as to the *Mechanician's* actual fate. After being torpedoed she was towed into the Needles Channel, grounded on the Shingles Bank south of Milford-on-Sea and abandoned. She broke in two later in the year and by the end of 1918 had become part buried. In 1922 the wreck was dispersed to seabed level by Trinity House.
On page 205 there are two errors concerning the *Diplomat*. She was completed in 1912, not 1904 and her engines were Q. 4-cyl, not T. 3-cyl. The caption to the photograph of the *Storsten* (page 211) should say March 1941, not March 1942.
There is a typographical error on page 235 where the name of the *Ngomei Chau* has been printed as *Ngomei Chou*. The caption to the photograph of the *Agios Georgios IV* on page 260 is wrong. The photograph was taken on 21 September 1938 (not 1939) when she was at Victoria, B.C. on a voyage from Vancouver to London, calling in at New Westminster, Victoria and Port Alberni.
BOB TODD, Head of Historic Photographs and Ship Plans Section, National Maritime Museum, Greenwich, London SE10 9NF

Does anyone know the function of the fitting on the bow of *Tactician* (page 198)? It may be a casting of some sort, possibly a temporary fitting, as it appears to be attached to the bow by wire strops.
A further observation, on page 231, *Chindwara* became *Kota Aman* and *Chantala* became *Kota Sentosa*.
I hope the proposed colour section proves a success. Just think what a a magnificent looking ship like the *Explorer* would look like if only colour ohotography had been available.
TONY SMYTHE, 35 Avondale Road, Rayleigh, Essex SS6 8NJ

There is a reasonable picture of *Huntsman* (1) (page 202) on page 812 of 'Shipping Wonders of the World' by Clarence Winchester. The name cannot be read in the picture, but Boer War hull number 125 should verify the ship's identity. *(Inspecting this photograph finds that it could well be the* Huntsman, *but is unlikely to show her as a Boer War transport as she was completed in 1904, two years after this war ended. Does any reader know the whereabouts of the original, or can loan us a good print? Ed.)*
Page 218 *Britannia*: '...the particularly prominent stay for her funnel'. I think that the 'stay' was of a temporary nature and clearly comprised a block and tackle. Surely it must have been a makeshift arrangement, rigged up during the sea trials because the funnel was vibrating excessively. Doubtless the funnel would be stiffened, or more adequately stayed before the *Britannia* entered service.

Page 219: '...fitted with a double-ended boiler which necessitated the second funnel'. I wonder if this was the real reason, or was the second funnel essentially cosmetic? In the case of a double-ended boiler, the two smoke outlets are usually combined into a single uptake and thence into a single funnel. In *Britannia*, space considerations above the boiler might have necessitated a different arrangement, but this would be unusual.
Page 232: *Kunak*: '...her Hawthorn Leslie engine was made in 1945 and only installed in *Baud* in 1949'. The type of engine in this case was a Werkspoor eight-cylinder, single-acting design, with under piston super-charge. Between about 1936 and 1948, the Hawthorn Leslie St. Peters engine works constructed nearly thirty identical engines of this design. Houlder Brothers had six engines fitted into three of their twin-screw refrigerated vessels, but the Anglo-Saxon Petroleum Co. (or Shell) were by far the main customers, the engines being installed in many 12,000 dwt. tankers built at Hebburn, but also some Anglo-Saxon tankers built at various other shipyards. It was said that because of the number of tankers with this type of machinery, Anglo-Saxon arranged for Hawthorn Leslie to keep one spare engine in stock. The last tanker to have an eight-cylinder Werkspoor engine was built about 1948 and thereafter Shell had other kinds of machinery installed in their new tankers. I believe that the *Baud's* engine was, in fact, the spare Shell engine, which was offered for sale, when the requirement to have a spare available no longer existed.
JOHN B. HILL, The Hollies, Wall, Hexham, Northumberland NE46 4EQ

Rowan's Russell list

With sorrow, we record the death early this year of Rowan Hackman at the age of 85. Most ship researchers, and especially those who are members of the World Ship Society, will know that Rowan's records of launch dates, yard numbers and other shipbuilding data were matched only by his generosity in sharing them with others. As well as Rowan's several articles in Record, *many of our fleet lists benefited from the information he supplied. Typical of Rowan's generosity was his spontaneous supply of information, such as the table below which includes yard numbers, tonnages and launch dates of all the sister hulls of the Russell-built* Beechbank, *which featured in* Record 14, *data which is reproduced as a tribute to a fellow researcher who will be greatly missed.*

No.	Name	Tonnage	Launched
217	STRATHGRYFE	2,276	5.2.1890
223	SIMLA	2,214	5.3.1890
239	GARNET HILL	2,274	15.4.1890
227	ELMBANK	2,288	26.3.1890
241	COMLIEBANK	2,283	2.9.1890
242	GOWANBANK	2,288	12.2.1891
243	HINEMOA	2,283	30.10.1890
244	PORT STANLEY	2,276	17.11.1890
265	EARL OF DUNMORE	2,257	14.5.1891
281	GLENOGIL	2,285	17.12.1891
282	LINDFIELD	2,280	2.11.1891
283	MAYFIELD	2,285	17.12.1891
285	JORDANHILL	2,291	4.2.1892
288	ASHBANK	2,292	20.11.1891
289	BEECHBANK	2,288	31.3.1892
294	DONNA FRANCISCA	2,130	29.2.1892
295	SOFALA	2,301	21.3.1892
300	KING JAMES	2,305	11.4.1892
303	ANCYRA	2,333	8.6.1892
312	SARATOGA	2,297	19.12.1892
323	KINROSS-SHIRE	2,299	2.5.1893
330	DOWANHILL	2,115	13.6.1893
339	BAHAMA	2,245	10.10.1893
340	CLAN GRAHAM	2,147	15.11.1893
341	KING GEORGE	2,242	28.11.1893
347	CLAN GALBRAITH	2,149	1.2.1894
348	FALLS OF ETTRICK	2,264	27.2.1894
357	GRENADA	2,268	26.10.1894
359	KING DAVID	2,240	10.5.1894
393	THORNLIEBANK	2,105	8.9.1896
402	AUSTRALIAN	2,103	25.12.1896

Four-master matters

May I add my two penn'orth to Stephen Howells' article on the Harrison four masted vessels? Unlike him, I was fortunate enough to actually see one of these vessels in her closing years, the *Defender*, anchored off the port of Beira awaiting a berth. This could often take in excess of two months, unless you were either (a) a mail and passenger liner such as *Llangibby Castle*, or (b) Portuguese. As I made three voyages in the intermediate, round-Africa service, the precise date cannot be recalled, but would certainly be between January and July 1950.

The *Explorer* had a bizarre encounter with a First World War U-boat on 6th February 1917, off Southern Ireland, when a torpedo fired from ahead hit her exactly 'head on' in her fore foot. Her stem was split up to anchor level, giving her the appearance of a bodged fitment of bow doors! This can be seen in a photograph published on page 1340 of part 42 of 'Shipping Wonders of the World', dated 24th November 1936. Needless to say, she survived such mistreatment.

ALAN PHIPPS, 2 Riverside Road, Droitwich Spa, Worcestershire WR9 8UW

HELP PUT IT ON RECORD

In this column we ask readers to help us locate elusive photographs or information to complete features planned for future issues of *Record*. Your help will make *Record* even more of a record.

For a feature on Thomas Skinner's Castles we are requesting photographs of this fleet. These are elusive, as the vessels were short-lived, but we hope that collectors, especially those in Australia, may be able to help or suggest sources for: *Gordon Castle* (1871-1900), *Drummond Castle* (1872-1873), *Braemar Castle* (1873-1880), *Cawdor Castle* (1873-1876), *Glamis Castle* (1874-1887, lost 1891 as Donaldson's *Circe*) *Fleurs Castle* (1874-1882); *Loudon Castle* (1877-1887, Italian *Marco Minghetti* until 1923), *Kenmure Castle* (1879-1883), *Bothwell Castle* (1881-1896, Australian *Coolgardie* until 1922), *Stirling Castle* (1882-1883, Italian *Nord America* until 1911), *Minard Castle* (1882-1883).

For a forthcoming book we would also like to hear from anyone who served with Athel and Orient Lines, United Baltic Corporation, Ramsey Steamship Co. Ltd. and Chellew S.N. Co. Ltd.

EVERY PICTURE TELLS A STORY

The story told by this photograph, kindly loaned by Kevin O'Donoghue, is not obvious, but the clues are very intriguing. A typical British steam coaster, built any time from the mid-1880s to 1914, appears to have come off her berth: note the rope draped over the counter in a rather unseamanlike fashion, the hatch covers off (suggesting she was discharging), and a broken rope ladder. The large number of soldiers aboard, including a number climbing the rigging, is notable. It puts the date during the First World War, and indicates that an army camp is nearby. The absence of civilians amongst the seven officers on the bridge suggests that the army may have been lending a hand during some sort of salvage operation, although activity around the bow suggests something more nautical in the way of repairs.

It is difficult to place the incident as, frustratingly, the nameboard on the shop on the quayside is partly obscured, but there is an east coast feel to the town. Indeed, the editor jumped to the conclusion that the coaster belonged to the Horlock family (who had funnels painted yellow with a black top, and occasionally had grey hulls) and that the scene might have been at their home port at Mistley. However, none of Horlock's coasters seem to fit the bill, and photographs of Mistley do not match the scene.

Photographs of ships, and especially coasters, where no name is visible and ownership unknown are notoriously hard to identify, and there are no helpful details on the back of the card. Nevertheless, it is hoped that readers may be able to identify the location, if not the particular ship or incident.